AJ & The Constellation of Kindness: A Guide to Holistic Wellness, Focus & Peace

AJ & The Constellation of Kindness: A Guide to Holistic Wellness, Focus & Peace

Companion Workbook Authored By:

Leigh Robertson, LCSW

THE SUNSHINE COLLABORATIVE

ISBN: 9798218769253

Important Disclaimer

The content provided in this workbook is for **educational and supportive purposes**. The skills and tools taught are intended as a form of **essential preventive care** to help children develop emotional regulation, resilience, and overall well-being. However, this workbook is not a substitute for professional mental health diagnosis or treatment. The activities and information are designed to support a child's holistic wellness and social-emotional learning, but they are not a replacement for guidance from a qualified mental health professional. If you have concerns about a child's emotional well-being, please consult with a qualified professional.

AJ & The Constellation of Kindness: A Guide to Holistic Wellness, Focus & Peace

Front Matter

- A Companion Guide — Page 1
- About the Author — Page 2

Part 1: Foundational Concepts

- I. Introduction for Educators & Caregiver — Page 3
    - The Heart of This Guide: Regulating Our Inner Universe
    - The Power of Practice
    - A Unique Benefit for Adults Too
    - How to Use This Workbook
- II. Core Wellness Concepts & How the Book Addresses Them — Page 6
    - Body Awareness & Nervous System Regulation
    - Emotional Literacy & Management
    - Mindful Awareness & Focus
    - Empathy & Connection
    - Resilience & Purposeful Action

Part 2: Chapter-by-Chapter Activity Guides

- III. Chapter 1: The Night the Stars Went Dim — Page 9
    - Discussion Questions
    - Staged Activities for Each Age Group
- III. Chapter 2: Lost in the Whispering Wood — Page 15
    - Discussion Questions
    - Staged Activities for Each Age Group
- III. Chapter 3: Destination: Planet of Anger — Page 21
    - Discussion Questions
    - Staged Activities for Each Age Group
- III. Chapter 4: The Weeping Willow and the Whispers of Sorrow — Page 29
    - Discussion Questions
    - Staged Activities for Each Age Group
- III. Chapter 5: The Starlight Singers and the Symphony of Hope — Page 35
    - Discussion Questions
    - Staged Activities for Each Age Group

- III. Chapter 6: Return to Cordium and the Kindness Ripple Effect Page 41
    - Discussion Questions
    - Staged Activities for Each Age Group

Part 3: Supplementary Materials

- Printable Handouts & Bonus Worksheets Reference List Page 46
- Appendix: All Printable Pages Page 50

A Companion Guide

This workbook is a special companion to the children's book, ***AJ & The Constellation of Kindness***, co-authored by Leigh Robertson, LCSW and her neurodiverse son. The book can be purchased through major booksellers and at **thesunshinecollaborative.com**. The activities and lessons within this guide are designed to be used with the book's story, which follows a young boy named AJ on a cosmic adventure to restore kindness and help creatures navigate their emotions.

For the best experience, we encourage you to use this workbook alongside the children's book. ***AJ and the Constellation of Kindness: A Guide to Holistic Wellness, Focus & Peace***, was created to go directly with the book, offering a flexible approach to incorporating the story's lessons into a classroom, counseling session, or home environment. This collaboration between a clinical social worker and her son is a testament to the power of emotional well-being, the healing nature of kindness, and is designed to inspire young readers to embrace their unique strengths.

Visit **thesunshinecollaborative.com** to discover more resources and connect with the author.

About the Author

As a mom of five and a licensed clinical social worker engaged in a Kentucky based private practice since 2008, **Leigh Robertson** brings a wealth of real-world experience to *AJ & the Constellation of Kindness.* She collaborated with her imaginative, neurodiverse son, AJ, to bring his vision to life, creating a heartwarming story that nurtures kindness and empathy in young readers.

Leigh believes in equipping children with the ability to understand and navigate their inner experiences. The book's techniques, such as purposeful breathing and grounding, are powerful, evidence-informed tools for regulating the nervous system, which she believes is the foundation for effective attention and academic success.

Beyond the lessons for children, Leigh believes that adults using the book and its companion workbook will also discover profound personal benefits, reinforcing their own regulation skills . The book's final message, **"You are amazing. Take care of YOU!"**, is a personal message that she hopes will resonate with readers of all ages, reminding them that the path to well-being is a lifelong journey.

I. Introduction for Educators & Caregivers

Welcome, incredible educators, dedicated caregivers, and compassionate guides! The activities and lessons within this workbook are organized according to the 'Absorb, Do, Connect' instructional design framework. This model, created by William Horton, categorizes learning activities to provide a balanced and intentional approach, ensuring that learners first absorb information, then actively practice new skills, and finally connect their learning to their lives.

We are thrilled to share *AJ & The Constellation of Kindness*, a unique journey co-created by a licensed clinical social worker and her imaginative neurodiverse son. This book invites children on a cosmic adventure while subtly integrating powerful tools for **holistic health and wellness**.

The Heart of This Guide: Regulating Our Inner Universe

In an increasingly complex world, equipping children with the ability to understand and navigate their inner experiences is more vital than ever. This workbook provides practical strategies that help children learn to regulate their **nervous system** – the body's control center for how we react to the world around us.

Think of it this way: When our bodies feel calm and regulated, our brains are optimally prepared for learning, creativity, and healthy social interaction. *AJ & The Constellation of Kindness* gently teaches children how to shift from states of overwhelm, worry, or frustration to states of calm, focus, and curiosity. The techniques woven into AJ's adventure — like purposeful breathing, grounding in the present moment, and gently shifting unhelpful thoughts — are powerful, evidence-informed tools for achieving this regulation. These are fundamental skills that contribute to a child's overall well-being, fostering resilience and adaptability that will serve them throughout their lives.

Crucially, when we learn to regulate our nervous system, we gain a profound **choice** in how we respond to our feelings and the world around us. Instead of simply reacting to intense emotions, we empower ourselves to pause, find calm, and **decide what we do next**. This inherent power of choice is ours to control, enabling us to act in ways that align with our values and lead to positive outcomes.

By strengthening their capacity for **body regulation and holistic wellness**, children enhance their ability to:

- **Concentrate and Engage in Learning:** A regulated nervous system is the foundation for effective attention and academic success.
- **Develop Core Life Skills:** They learn to respond thoughtfully rather than react impulsively, essential for problem-solving and navigating challenges.
- **Build Strong, Positive Relationships:** Understanding and managing one's own internal state allows for greater empathy and more harmonious interactions with others.
- **Cultivate Future-Ready Qualities:** These foundational skills equip children to become adaptable, resilient, and thriving individuals, preparing them to excel in educational systems and contribute positively in future employment and community roles. This is truly good for all children, preparing them to navigate a dynamic future with confidence and inner strength.

The Power of Practice:

It is essential to remember that cultivating these skills requires consistent practice. Just like learning to read, ride a bike, or play a musical instrument, nervous system regulation and conscious emotional responses become stronger and more automatic with repetition. The activities within this workbook are designed to be revisited and integrated into daily routines, transforming moments of learning into lifelong habits for well-being.

A Unique Benefit for Adults Too:

While *AJ & The Constellation of Kindness* is designed for children, we firmly believe that **adults using this book and workbook with younger populations will also discover profound personal benefits**. As you guide children through activities like purposeful breathing, grounding, and letting go of unhelpful thoughts, you may find yourself **learning, being reminded of, or reinforcing your own personal regulation skills**. Co-author Leigh Robertson, a seasoned clinician and mother, continually finds these practices invaluable in her own life, recognizing their universal applicability. This workbook offers a shared growth experience, fostering greater calm and resilience not just for the child, but for the adult facilitator as well. It's a powerful reminder that the path to well-being is a lifelong journey, relevant across all ages and stages of life.

How to Use This Workbook:

This guide offers a flexible approach to incorporating the wisdom of *AJ & The Constellation of Kindness* into your classroom, counseling sessions, or home environment. We encourage a "Staged Learning" progression, where activities are tied directly to the book's chapters, allowing children to build skills incrementally. You'll find:

- **Age-Adapted Activities:** Suggestions for "Young Explorers" (Grades K-2) and "Middle Navigators" (Grades 3-5), with tips for further adaptation.
- **Ready-to-Use Printables:** Copy pages to save you time and enhance engagement.
- **Facilitator Tips:** Guidance for leading discussions and activities effectively.

Important Note: The content provided in this workbook is for educational and supportive purposes. It is not intended as a substitute for professional mental health diagnosis or treatment. If you have concerns about a child's emotional well-being, please consult with a qualified professional.

II. Core Wellness Concepts & How the Book Addresses Them

AJ & The Constellation of Kindness is built upon foundational principles that contribute to a child's overall well-being and their ability to navigate life's experiences with greater ease and resilience. While the narrative is a fantastical journey, the underlying mechanisms for growth are deeply rooted in understanding our inner world and how it connects to our physical body. These are core components of holistic wellness:

1. **Body Awareness & Nervous System Regulation:**
   - **Concept:** This involves tuning into the physical sensations within the body and learning strategies to shift from states of stress or overwhelm (e.g., fight, flight, freeze responses) to states of calm, focus, and safety. A regulated nervous system is crucial for optimal learning, emotional balance, and physical health.
   - **How the Book Addresses It:** AJ learns to recognize his own physical reactions (like the tingling sensation or feeling uneasy) and actively uses tools like purposeful breathing and grounding techniques to calm his body and mind (e.g., with the Worrions on the Planet of Fear). This demonstrates how conscious engagement with our body can bring inner peace.
2. **Emotional Literacy & Management:**
   - **Concept:** The ability to identify, understand, and constructively express one's own emotions, as well as to recognize and respond empathetically to the emotions of others. It's about knowing what we feel and having tools to navigate those feelings effectively.
   - **How the Book Addresses It:** AJ encounters creatures embodying different "big" emotions (fearful Worrions, fiery Flamma, sorrowful Pluvia). Through his interactions, he models and teaches ways to name feelings, process them, and choose healthier responses, rather than being overwhelmed by them (e.g., using a calm voice on the Planet of Anger, letting go of sad thoughts on the Planet of Sadness).
3. **Mindful Awareness & Focus:**
   - **Concept:** The practice of paying attention to the present moment without judgment. This enhances concentration, reduces distraction, and helps individuals connect more deeply with their experiences.
   - **How the Book Addresses It:** Techniques like the "5-4-3-2-1" sensory game prompt AJ (and readers) to focus on immediate sensory input, redirecting attention away from overwhelming thoughts or external distractions and

bringing them back to the present moment. This cultivation of present-moment awareness fosters mental clarity.

4. **Empathy & Connection:**
    - **Concept:** The capacity to understand or feel what another person is experiencing from their frame of reference. It involves recognizing and sharing the feelings of others, fostering compassionate relationships and a sense of belonging.
    - **How the Book Addresses It:** AJ's entire mission is driven by empathy for the dimming Cordium and the distressed creatures he meets. He actively listens to their struggles and offers support tailored to their needs, demonstrating how understanding and compassion can create positive "ripple effects" and strengthen community bonds.
5. **Resilience & Purposeful Action:**
    - **Concept:** The ability to recover quickly from difficulties, adapt to change, and persevere in the face of challenges. It involves developing a sense of agency and making constructive choices that align with one's well-being and positive contributions.
    - **How the Book Addresses It:** Despite moments of doubt, AJ continues his mission, demonstrating courage and determination. He takes purposeful action to help others, ultimately restoring Cordium and leaving a lasting positive impact, reinforcing the idea that even small acts of kindness and self-care contribute to a greater purpose.

III. Chapter-by-Chapter Activity Guides

Chapter 1: The Night the Stars Went Dim

- **Core Emotional Theme(s):** Introducing Worry/Unease; Discovering Inner Guidance
- **Book Synopsis:** AJ enjoys a peaceful night stargazing with his mom until the beloved constellation Cordium, a majestic heart-shaped constellation, begins to dim. A shimmering light and a mysterious voice call upon AJ for help, giving him a magical Compass of Compassion and introducing him to his whimsical guide, Whimsy, for a cosmic mission to restore kindness.
- **Key Regulation & Wellness Concepts Introduced:**
    - Recognizing the physical sensations of worry or unease in the body.
    - Understanding the concept of an "inner compass" or intuition as a source of personal guidance.
    - Introducing basic purposeful breathing to calm the nervous system.
    - Introducing grounding to feel stable and present.

Discussion Questions

For Young Explorers (Grades K-2):

- Before Reading: "What does it feel like in your body when you're a little worried or nervous? Where do you feel it? (e.g., fluttery tummy, tight shoulders)."
- After Reading: "What was the 'Constellation of Kindness' called, and what happened to it? How do you think AJ felt when it started to dim?"
- After Reading: "AJ got a special compass that glowed with a warm, golden light. What do you think that compass helped him do?"
- After Reading: "What did the voice tell AJ he needed to do to help Cordium? How do you think he felt about that mission?"

For Middle Navigators (Grades 3-5):

- Before Reading: "Think about a time you felt a big emotion, maybe worry or excitement. How did your body feel? What sensations did you notice?"
- After Reading: "The 'Constellation of Kindness' started to dim. What do you think that might symbolize about kindness in the universe or even in our own lives? What do you think could cause a 'constellation of kindness' to dim?"
- After Reading: "AJ received a 'Compass of Compassion.' What do you think 'compassion' means? How might a compass that guides with compassion be different from a regular compass?"

- After Reading: "AJ felt a tingling sensation and heard a voice. What do you think that might represent about listening to our inner feelings or intuition? How might your 'inner compass' communicate with you?"

Staged Activities for Each Age Group

A. Young Explorers (Grades K-2)

1. **Activity: Listening for Our Feelings (Absorb)**
    - **Objective(s):** To help children identify basic body sensations associated with emotions, especially unease or excitement. This is a foundational step in body awareness and nervous system regulation.
    - **Materials:** None needed.
    - **Instructions:**
        - Have children sit comfortably. Say, "Just like AJ felt a tingling sensation, sometimes our bodies tell us how we're feeling. Our body is like a wise helper, sending us messages."
        - Guide them: "Close your eyes if you like, or soften your gaze. Let's imagine we're about to go on an exciting adventure, just like AJ. Take a moment to notice... where do you feel that excitement in your body? (Pause for responses: maybe butterflies in the tummy, fast heart, wiggles)."
        - "Now, let's imagine something feels a little quiet or worried, like the dimming stars. Where do you feel *that* in your body? (Pause: maybe shoulders feel tight, tummy feels squishy, a sigh)."
        - "Thank your body for telling you how it feels. All feelings and all body messages are okay. Our bodies are very smart!"
    - **Facilitator Tips:** Keep it light and non-judgmental. Emphasize that all feelings are part of our experience. This is a gentle introduction to interoception (awareness of internal body states).
2. **Activity: Belly Breathing Buddies (Do)**
    - **Objective(s):** To introduce and practice simple, calming diaphragmatic breathing, a key tool for nervous system regulation.
    - **Materials:** One small, lightweight **stuffed animal or favorite small toy** per child.
    - **Instructions:**
        - Have children lie on their backs on the floor or a mat.

        - "Place your belly buddy [or 'small toy'] on your tummy, right where AJ's tummy might have felt fluttery when he got the compass."
        - "Now, take a slow, gentle breath in through your nose, and watch your belly buddy rise up towards the sky. Like your tummy is a balloon filling with air."
        - "Then, slowly let the air out through your mouth, and watch your belly buddy gently fall back down. Like letting the air out of the balloon."
        - Repeat 3-5 times. "Notice how your belly buddy goes up and down with your breath. Your breath is a powerful tool to help your body feel calm and quiet, just like it helped AJ prepare for his big journey."
    - **Facilitator Tips:** Model the breathing clearly. Use a soft, calming voice. Emphasize the visual of the rising and falling buddy to keep them engaged. Remind them they can use their own hand as a belly buddy anytime.
    - **Printable Page Reference:** "My Belly Buddy Breath Visual".
3. **Activity: My Inner Sparkle (Connect)**
    - **Objective(s):** To help children connect with their own sense of inner strength and goodness, fostering self-awareness and positive self-perception, similar to AJ's "Compass of Compassion."
    - **Materials:** Paper, crayons/colored pencils/markers.
    - **Instructions:**
        - "AJ's Compass of Compassion glowed with a warm light, guiding him. We all have a special 'inner sparkle' inside us – our own goodness, kindness, and bravery that guides us and helps us shine."
        - "On your paper, draw what your 'inner sparkle' looks like. It could be a color, a shape, a symbol, or anything you imagine. Show how bright it shines inside you!"
        - Optional: Share drawings. "What makes your inner sparkle shine brightest? How does it feel when your inner sparkle is shining?"
    - **Facilitator Tips:** Validate all drawings and ideas. Encourage children to think about actions or qualities that make them feel strong, kind, or good inside.
    - **Printable Page Reference:** "My Inner Sparkle Drawing Page" (or "My Inner Sparkle Boy Writing Lines" , "My Inner Sparkle Girl Writing Lines" , "My Inner Sparkle Heart Drawing Space" as alternatives).

B. Middle Navigators (Grades 3-5)

1. **Activity: My Body's "Feeling Detector" (Absorb)**
    - **Objective(s):** To deepen awareness of physiological responses to different emotional states, understanding how the nervous system communicates and influences physical sensations.
    - **Materials:** Whiteboard/chart paper, markers.
    - **Instructions:**
        - "AJ felt powerful sensations when the light enveloped him, and throughout his journey, his body reacted to different planets and emotions. Our bodies are amazing 'feeling detectors' that send us messages about our internal state."
        - "Let's make a class list. What are some of the physical sensations your body might send when you're feeling:
            - **Excited or super ready for something?** (e.g., heart thumping, restless, tingly, wide eyes, quick breath)
            - **A little worried or nervous?** (e.g., knot in stomach, tight shoulders, shaky hands, racing thoughts, shallow breath)
            - **Calm or peaceful?** (e.g., relaxed muscles, slow, steady breath, light feeling, clear head)"
        - "Notice how different feelings often have different body messages. When we pay attention to these messages, we can start to understand our own inner universe and how our nervous system is doing."
    - **Facilitator Tips:** Encourage specific, descriptive words. Reinforce that these are normal body responses, and knowing them helps us choose strategies. This activity builds vocabulary for internal states and connection to nervous system activity.
2. **Activity: Cosmic Calming Breath & Grounding (Do)**
    - **Objective(s):** To practice two foundational nervous system regulation techniques (deep breathing and grounding) in combination, providing tools for stability and calm.
    - **Materials:** None needed.
    - **Instructions:**
        - "AJ's Compass of Compassion was his guide. Our breath can be like a compass, guiding our body back to calm. Our feet can be like anchors,

keeping us steady and present, especially when our nervous system feels overwhelmed."

        - **Part 1: Cosmic Calming Breath:** "Sit or stand tall. We're going to do a slow, deep breath, like tracing the points of a star. Breathe in slowly through your nose for a count of 4. Hold briefly for a count of 2. Breathe out slowly through your mouth for a count of 6. Let all the air out, feeling your stomach gently go in. Repeat 3-5 times. Notice how your breath can help your body feel more regulated and calm, like the vast, peaceful cosmos."
        - **Part 2: Grounding with Roots:** "Now, place your feet flat on the floor, noticing the contact. Really feel them there. Imagine strong, deep roots growing from the bottoms of your feet, digging deep into the earth, making you feel incredibly stable and connected. You are strong and steady, just like a mighty tree."
        - **Combine:** "As you do your Cosmic Calming Breath, feel your roots growing deeper with each exhale, anchoring you firmly in place. This helps your nervous system feel safe and secure."
    - **Facilitator Tips:** Model the counting and the physical actions. Remind them these are portable tools they can use any time they need to feel more steady or calm, helping their nervous system settle. Encourage them to visualize the star as they breathe.
    - **Printable Page Reference:** "Cosmic Calming Breath & Grounding Visual".
3. **Activity: My Inner Guide Journal (Connect)**
    - **Objective(s):** To encourage self-reflection on inner guidance, intuition, and how personal values can direct positive choices and well-being.
    - **Materials:** Journal pages (from workbook or blank paper), pens/pencils.
    - **Instructions:**
        - "AJ's Compass of Compassion glowed and guided him on his adventure. We all have an 'inner guide' – a sense of what feels right, what's kind, or what we truly need for our own well-being. Sometimes it's a quiet voice, a gut feeling, or a strong sense of knowing that helps our nervous system feel more settled when we listen to it."
        - **Journal Prompts:** Choose one or two for students to reflect on and write about:

        - "What do you think *your* inner guide or 'inner compass' feels like or tells you when you're making a choice about your actions or how you feel?"
        - "Think of a time you followed your inner guide, even if it was a small decision (e.g., choosing to take a break, asking for help, being kind). What happened, and how did it make you feel physically and emotionally?"
        - "If your inner guide could give you one message about kindness, courage, or taking care of yourself for the week, what would it say? How would listening to that message benefit your own health and wellness?"
    - Optional: Share thoughts in pairs or small groups, emphasizing that everyone's inner guide might feel or sound different.
- **Facilitator Tips:** Emphasize that there are no "right" or "wrong" answers. Encourage honest reflection and validate their unique experiences. This activity helps connect abstract concepts to personal experience and the benefits of listening to one's internal cues.
- **Printable Page Reference:** "My Inner Guide Journal Page".

Chapter 2: Lost in the Whispering Woods

- **Core Emotional Theme(s):** Navigating Worry & Fear; Harnessing Sensory Awareness for Regulation.
- **Book Synopsis:** AJ and Whimsy land on the mysterious Planet of Fear, where "Whispers of Worry" try to overwhelm them. As the ground shifts into a confusing maze, AJ recalls his mom's teachings, using deep breathing, grounding, and a special "5-4-3-2-1" sensory game to regain his focus. He then shares these powerful tools to help the frightened "Worrions" find their courage, bringing more light back to Cordium.
- **Key Regulation & Wellness Concepts Introduced:**
    - The overwhelming nature of fear and worry, and how it can affect perception.
    - Deep breathing and grounding as anchors for nervous system regulation in moments of intensity.
    - Using sensory awareness ("5-4-3-2-1" game) to reorient and calm the nervous system when feeling overwhelmed or distracted.
    - Finding an "inner quiet space" for comfort and calm.
    - The power of shared experience and connection in managing difficult emotions.

Discussion Questions

For Young Explorers (Grades K-2):

- Before Reading: "When you feel worried, do you ever feel like there are 'whispers' or tricky thoughts in your head? What do they sound like?"
- After Reading: "What were the 'Whispers of Worry' trying to tell AJ? How did they make him feel?"
- After Reading: "AJ used some special tricks from his mom when the whispers got loud. What were some of those tricks? How did they help him feel steadier?"
- After Reading: "AJ helped the Worrions learn tricks too. Why was it important for him to share what he knew?"

For Middle Navigators (Grades 3-5):

- Before Reading: "Have you ever felt 'lost' in your thoughts or emotions, like you couldn't find your way through a tricky situation? What was that like?"

- After Reading: "The 'Whispers of Worry' seemed to feed on fear. How do our own worries sometimes grow bigger when we focus on them? What did AJ do to stop feeding them?"
- After Reading: "AJ used a '5-4-3-2-1' game. How do you think focusing on senses helps your nervous system calm down when you're feeling overwhelmed or panicky?"
- After Reading: "When AJ helped the Worrions, how did that also help him? What does that teach us about connecting with others who are struggling?"

Staged Activities for Each Age Group

A. Young Explorers (Grades K-2)

1. **Activity: The Worry Maze (Absorb)**
   - **Objective(s):** To visually represent how worry can feel confusing and to introduce the idea of finding a path through it.
   - **Materials:** Large paper or whiteboard, markers.
   - **Instructions:**
     - "In the story, AJ found himself in a confusing maze in the Whispering Woods, where the Whispers of Worry made things feel even trickier."
     - "Let's imagine a worry maze. On the paper, I'll draw some squiggly lines that look like a maze. As I draw, think about how worry can make your brain feel mixed up."
     - "Now, let's draw a clear path through the maze. What helps us find a clear path when our brains feel squiggly with worries? (Guide responses towards things like deep breaths, thinking calmly, asking for help, just like AJ did)."
   - **Facilitator Tips:** Keep the drawing simple and focus on the feeling of confusion and then the clarity of a path. Emphasize that finding a way through is possible.
2. **Activity: My Body Anchor & Rainbow Breathing (Do)**
   - **Objective(s):** To actively practice grounding and deep breathing as a combined nervous system regulation strategy when feeling shaky or overwhelmed.
   - **Materials:** None needed.
   - **Instructions:**

        - "AJ learned to feel his feet on the ground even when it was icy and shifting. That's called 'grounding,' and it helps our body feel anchored and safe."
        - "Stand up. Put your feet flat on the floor like strong roots. Now, imagine a giant rainbow arching over you. We'll breathe in and trace the rainbow with our arms."
        - "Breathe in slowly through your nose as your arms go up, drawing the first color of the rainbow. Breathe out slowly through your mouth as your arms come down. Feel your feet firmly on the ground. Repeat for each color, feeling anchored and calm with each breath."
        - "Notice how your feet feel strong on the ground. This helps your body feel safe and settled."
    - **Facilitator Tips:** Model the movements clearly. Use a calm, steady voice. Emphasize the feeling of stability in their feet.
    - **Printable Page Reference:** "Rainbow Breath & Body Anchor Visual."
3. **Activity: My Quiet Space Drawing (Connect)**
    - **Objective(s):** To encourage children to identify and visualize a personal safe and calm internal space, a tool for self-soothing and regulation.
    - **Materials:** Paper, crayons/colored pencils/markers.
    - **Instructions:**
        - "When things got loud and confusing, Whimsy told AJ to remember his 'quiet space' – his hammock. We all have a place where we feel safe, calm, and peaceful, even if it's just in our imagination."
        - "Close your eyes if you like, and imagine *your* quiet space. What does it look like? What colors are there? What sounds or smells? How does your body feel when you are there?"
        - "Now, on your paper, draw your quiet space. This is your special place to go in your mind whenever you need to feel calm and settled."
        - Optional: Share their drawings briefly, focusing on the feelings evoked.
    - **Facilitator Tips:** Emphasize that this is an *imagined* space, accessible anytime. Validate all ideas of a quiet space (could be real or fantastical).
    - **Printable Page Reference:** "My Quiet Space Drawing Page".

B. Middle Navigators (Grades 3-5)

1. **Activity: Decoding the Whispers (Absorb)**
   - **Objective(s):** To help students recognize how worried thoughts (internal "whispers") can sound and affect their nervous system and actions.
   - **Materials:** Whiteboard/chart paper, markers.
   - **Instructions:**
     - "On the Planet of Fear, the Whispers of Worry tried to convince AJ he wasn't brave enough. Our own worries sometimes have 'voices' in our heads."
     - "Let's brainstorm: If worry could 'whisper' in your head, what might it say? (e.g., 'You'll fail,' 'Nobody likes you,' 'This is too hard,' 'You'll look silly')."
     - "How does hearing these 'whispers' make your body feel? (e.g., tense, tired, fluttery, heavy). This is your nervous system reacting to those thoughts."
     - "What might a 'compass of kindness' whisper back? (e.g., 'You are brave,' 'Try your best,' 'You've got this,' 'It's okay to make mistakes')."
   - **Facilitator Tips:** Frame this as an observation exercise, not a judgment. Emphasize that thoughts are just thoughts, and we can choose which "whispers" to listen to, which helps regulate our nervous system.
2. **Activity: The 5-4-3-2-1 Power Up (Do)**
   - **Objective(s):** To actively practice a sensory-based grounding technique for nervous system regulation, especially effective when feeling overwhelmed, anxious, or unfocused.
   - **Materials:** None needed.
   - **Instructions:**
     - "When the Whispers of Worry got too loud and confusing, AJ used the '5-4-3-2-1' game to calm his nervous system and refocus. This technique brings us back to the present moment, which helps settle our internal 'alarm system'."
     - "Let's try it together. Sit comfortably, feet on the floor. Look around the room (or wherever you are).
       - **5:** Name **5 things you can see**. (Pause for individual observation).

                ■ **4:** Name **4 things you can touch** right now. (Pause. Encourage feeling textures).
                ■ **3:** Name **3 things you can hear**. (Pause. Encourage listening for subtle sounds).
                ■ **2:** Name **2 things you can smell**. (Pause. This might be harder, accept "nothing").
                ■ **1:** Name **1 thing you can taste**. (Pause. This might be harder, accept "nothing" or "my toothpaste")."
        - "How does your body feel now? Notice how your nervous system can calm down when you bring your attention to your senses."
    - **Facilitator Tips:** Lead slowly. Encourage quiet, internal observation. Repeat a few times if needed. Explain that this is a portable tool for any time they feel overwhelmed or need to focus.
    - **Printable Page Reference:** "My 5-4-3-2-1 Power Up Checklist."

3. **Activity: My Sunshine Explorer Courage Shield (Connect)**
    - **Objective(s):** To help students visually represent their inner strengths and coping strategies as a protective force against worries, fostering resilience and personal agency.
    - **Materials:** Paper, crayons/colored pencils/markers.
    - **Instructions:**
        - "AJ learned he was braver than he thought, and he helped the Worrions find *their* courage. We all have inner courage and ways we protect ourselves from worries, like a shield, or like the powerful Sunshine Explorer spaceship that carries AJ safely through space!"
        - "On your 'My Sunshine Explorer Courage Shield' page, you'll see the outline of a shield that also looks like AJ's spaceship. Use different sections or 'windows' on the shield to draw symbols or small pictures that represent:
            - Your **Strengths** or things you're good at.
            - Things that make you feel **Brave** or safe.
            - **Ways you calm your body** when worries try to sneak in (like Cosmic Calming Breath or 5-4-3-2-1).
            - A **Goal** you have for yourself."
        - "This shield is a reminder of your inner power to face challenges and explore your own inner universe!"

- Optional: Share their shield designs and explain one symbol they chose.

- **Facilitator Tips:** Encourage creativity and personalization. Emphasize that the "shield" is internal – the skills and strengths they possess. Guide them in dividing the shield into sections for their drawings.
- **Printable Page Reference:** "My Sunshine Explorer Courage Shield Template".

Chapter 3: Destination: Planet of Anger

- **Core Emotional Theme(s):** Understanding & Navigating Anger; Practicing Calm Communication and Conscious Choice for Nervous System Regulation.
- **Book Synopsis:** AJ and Whimsy journey to the vibrant, volcanic Planet of Anger, home to the fiery Flamma whose emotions erupt like the very land they inhabit. As tensions rise and the volcano rumbles, AJ remembers his past lessons on regulation and courage. He learns that responding with a calm voice can cool down intense situations and discovers that connecting with the source of the anger, represented by a glowing crystal, can bring peace back to the planet and its inhabitants.
- **Key Regulation & Wellness Concepts Introduced:**
    - Identifying the physical sensations of anger in the body and recognizing anger as built-up energy/pressure.
    - The difference between uncontrolled "eruptions" and purposeful, regulated release of intense feelings, emphasizing the **power of a pause**.
    - The power of conscious **choice** in how we respond to intense emotions and external situations.
    - The impact of calm communication and tone of voice in de-escalating heightened situations, influencing one's own and others' nervous systems.
    - Using purposeful breathing to regulate one's own nervous system when anger is present.
    - The concept of finding and addressing the "source" of intense feelings to promote holistic balance.

Discussion Questions

For Young Explorers (Grades K-2):

- Before Reading: "When you feel really mad or frustrated, how does your body feel? Does it feel hot like a volcano, or shaky, or tight? Where do you notice it most?"
- After Reading: "What were the Flamma like on the Planet of Anger? How did they show they were angry?"
- After Reading: "AJ used a calm voice even when the Flamma were angry. Why do you think using a calm voice helps cool things down, instead of making them hotter? What **choice** did AJ make with his voice?"
- After Reading: "AJ helped the volcano calm down by touching a glowing crystal. What do you think that crystal means for our own big feelings – is there something inside

us that can help us calm down? And what **choice** can we make when we feel that power?"

For Middle Navigators (Grades 3-5):

- Before Reading: "Have you ever noticed how sometimes one person's anger can seem to make others around them feel angry too? What's that like? How does that 'energy' spread? Do you feel like you have a **choice** in how you respond when someone else is angry?"
- After Reading: "AJ observed that when one Flamma yelled, others yelled louder, like a chain reaction. How did AJ's approach of using a calm voice change that 'chain reaction'? What **choice** did AJ make that helped change the situation?"
- After Reading: "The crystal at the heart of the volcano seemed to fuel the Flamma's anger. How might this symbolize what happens when we hold onto our anger or don't address its root cause in our own bodies? What **choice** can we make about letting go of that built-up energy?"
- After Reading: "How do you think practicing calm communication, as AJ taught the Flamma, helps to regulate not only your own nervous system but also the nervous systems of those around you? Why is having the **choice** to communicate calmly so powerful?"

Staged Activities for Each Age Group

A. Young Explorers (Grades K-2)

1. **Activity: My Inner Volcano Eruption (Absorb - Demonstration & Discussion)**
    - **Objective(s):** To visually and kinetically demonstrate how anger can build up like pressure and lead to an uncontrolled "eruption," linking it to internal body sensations. This sets the stage for understanding **choice** in reaction.
    - **Materials:** Small plastic bottle or cup, baking soda, vinegar, dish soap (optional for more foam), tray or plastic bin for containment, food coloring (red/orange, optional).
    - **Instructions:**
        - "In the story, the Planet of Anger had volcanoes that erupted when the Flamma got angry. Our anger can sometimes build up like a volcano inside us, creating lots of hot energy."

        - **Demonstration:** (Perform a simple baking soda and vinegar volcano.) "Watch what happens when the pressure builds up inside the volcano! Boom! It's messy, right?"
        - **Discussion:** "When our anger builds up inside, it can feel like that volcano is about to erupt in our bodies. Where do you feel that 'hot volcano' feeling in your body? (e.g., face gets hot, fists clench, tummy feels tight)."
        - "Do we want our anger to explode like this volcano and make a big mess that's hard to clean up?" (Guide to 'no'). "So, we need ways to let some steam out safely, before it erupts. This shows we have a **choice** in how our anger comes out."
    - **Facilitator Tips:** Ensure a safe, contained space for the demonstration. Emphasize the *feeling* of pressure building and the *consequences* of an uncontrolled release versus making a **choice** for a safer release. Connect the visual to the idea of nervous system activation.
    - **Printable Page Reference:** "My Anger Volcano Drawing Page".
2. **Activity: Cool-Down Breath & Shake It Out (Do)**
    - **Objective(s):** To practice physical ways to release pent-up energy and calming breathing, regulating the nervous system before an "eruption," highlighting the **choice** to manage energy.
    - **Materials:** None (optional: soft scarves or streamers for "steam").
    - **Instructions:**
        - "After watching the volcano erupt, we know we have a **choice** to let our anger steam out in a safe way. AJ taught the Flamma to calm down with their breath."
        - **Part 1: Shake It Out:** "When you feel that hot volcano energy building, sometimes our body needs to move that energy out! Let's shake it out! Shake your hands, shake your feet, shake your whole body gently. Shake out that extra energy, like a dog shaking off water!" (Allow brief, safe movement).
        - **Part 2: Cool-Down Breath:** "Now, let's use our breath to cool down our volcano. Take a big breath in through your nose, imagining you're smelling a cool, calm breeze. Now, slowly blow out through your mouth, like you're gently blowing on a hot soup or making soft steam come out of your volcano. Feel the cool air on your lips. This helps blow out some of that hot, angry feeling and calms your nervous system."

        - Repeat 3-5 times. "Notice how your body feels more settled after moving and breathing. Remember, this is your **choice** to help your body calm down."
    - **Facilitator Tips:** Model the shaking and breathing. Emphasize that movement can release energy, and breath brings calm. Link it directly to helping the 'inner volcano' cool down, and empower children by highlighting their **choice** to use these tools.
    - **Printable Page Reference:** "Cool-Down Breath Visual".
3. **Activity: My Calm Voice Superpower (Connect)**
    - **Objective(s):** To introduce the concept that a calm tone of voice is a powerful tool that helps regulate both the speaker's and listener's nervous systems, stemming from a conscious **choice**.
    - **Materials:** None.
    - **Instructions:**
        - "When the Flamma were yelling, AJ used a calm voice. This was his superpower to help them start to listen and feel less angry. Our voice can be a special tool to help calm ourselves and others. We have a **choice** in how we use our voice."
        - "Let's practice! Say, 'I want that toy!' in a loud, stompy, angry voice. (Allow brief practice). How does that feel in *your* body when you yell? How might it make someone else's body feel? Does it invite a calm **choice** from them?"
        - "Now, take a 'Cool-Down Breath.' And then, say, 'I want that toy' in a calm, clear, even voice. How does *that* feel in your body? Which voice do you think helps others listen better and keeps everyone's nervous system calmer? Which **choice** feels better for you?"
        - "Practice a few times with different simple phrases (e.g., 'My turn,' 'I need help,' 'I don't like that'). Notice how keeping your voice calm helps your nervous system stay regulated too, and sends a signal of safety to others, inviting them to make a calm **choice**."
    - **Facilitator Tips:** Keep it playful but emphasize the physical and relational difference. Explicitly state that using a calm voice is a **choice** we make that influences ourselves and others.
    - **Printable Page Reference:** "Calm Voice, Loud Voice Visual".

B. Middle Navigators (Grades 3-5)

1. **Activity: The Power of the Pause: Two Sodas Demo (Absorb - Demonstration & Discussion)**
    - **Objective(s):** To vividly demonstrate how internal "pressure" builds with intense emotions like anger, and how taking a **pause** allows for nervous system regulation, enabling a conscious **choice** for a more controlled and positive response.
    - **Materials:** Two identical, unopened cans or plastic bottles of soda (e.g., carbonated water, juice, or regular soda), a safe, contained opening area (e.g., over a sink or large tray).
    - **Instructions:**
        - "The Planet of Anger was full of fiery energy. Sometimes, when we feel intense emotions like anger, it's like pressure building up inside us, just like shaking a soda can."
        - **Demonstration:**
            - "Let's call this Soda A. I'm going to shake it vigorously, creating a lot of internal 'emotional pressure.' (Shake Soda A for 10-15 seconds). Notice the bubbles and tension inside."
            - "Now, let's call this Soda B. I'm going to shake it just as much. (Shake Soda B vigorously for 10-15 seconds)."
            - "I'm going to open Soda A right away, without any pause. What do you predict will happen?" (Open Soda A quickly, allowing it to spray). "Woah! That was a messy, uncontrolled release of pressure! Sometimes, when we don't take a pause, our anger can come out like that, making a big mess that's hard to clean up."
            - "Now, Soda B has just as much 'anger pressure' inside. But instead of opening it right away, I'm going to take a **pause**. I'm going to let it sit for a moment, and I'll even gently tap the top a few times to help the bubbles settle. (Let Soda B sit for 30-60 seconds, gently tapping). This is like taking a deep breath or finding your inner calm."
            - "What do you predict will happen if I open Soda B now, after taking a pause?" (Open Soda B slowly and gently). "See? Same pressure, but because we took a **pause** and allowed the internal

system to settle, we had the **choice** for a much calmer, cleaner release!"

        - **Discussion:** "Our anger can feel like that shaken can. When we pause, even for a moment, it gives our nervous system a chance to settle. This pause gives us the **choice** to respond thoughtfully instead of just reacting. What are your own 'early warning signs' – the clues your body gives you that your internal 'pressure' is building? When you notice those signs, remember you have the power of **pause**, and the **choice** in how you respond next."
    - **Facilitator Tips:** Ensure safety during the demonstration. Emphasize the metaphor of internal pressure, early warnings, and the crucial **power of the pause** and subsequent **choice** for controlled release. This is a very memorable demonstration for this age group.
    - **Printable Page Reference:** "My Anger Thermometer & Warning Signs" (for students to identify their own pressure build-up and note their chosen pause strategies).
2. **Activity: The Calm Communication Switch (Do)**
    - **Objective(s):** To practice consciously choosing a regulated, calm tone of voice and body language in potentially aggravating situations, influencing one's own and others' nervous systems, and asserting **choice** in communication.
    - **Materials:** Scenario cards ("Calm Communication Scenario Cards").
    - **Instructions:**
        - "AJ observed that the Flamma's anger was contagious. But he figured out that his calm voice could be a 'switch' to change the energy, allowing for a more controlled 'release' of pressure, just like our settled soda can. We have a **choice** in how we communicate, and that choice can make a big difference."
        - "In pairs, take a scenario card. First, one person will say their angry reaction, as if they *didn't* use their calm switch or take a pause. The other person just listens and notices how it feels in their body to hear that, and how it might make them want to react without a **choice**."
        - "Then, take a few Cosmic Calming Breaths, like a short **pause** for your nervous system. Now, the same person says their reaction again, but this time, they consciously flip their 'calm communication switch' – using a calm voice, steady eye contact, and calm body language. The

other person notices the difference in their own body as they listen, and how it might invite them to make a calm **choice** too."
    - Swap roles.
  - **Facilitator Tips:** Stress that this is practice, not perfection. Debrief after each pair: "What did it feel like in your body when you used a calm voice versus a loud one?" "What was it like to hear a calm voice instead of an angry one? How did it impact your nervous system, and your **choice** of response?" Explicitly connect the calm response to making a conscious **choice** after a pause.

3. **Activity: Finding My Core Calm (Connect)**
  - **Objective(s):** To guide students in identifying an internal "calm core" or "peace crystal" that they can access for nervous system regulation, similar to AJ calming the volcano's core. This reinforces their capacity for conscious **choice** in seeking inner peace.
  - **Materials:** Paper, crayons/colored pencils/markers.
  - **Instructions:**
    - "AJ found a glowing crystal at the heart of the volcano that brought peace to the whole planet. We all have a 'core calm' inside us, a place of peace we can access, even when things around us are fiery and our internal pressure is high. This 'core calm' helps us make a **choice** to regulate our nervous system, especially after taking a **pause**."
    - "Take a few Cosmic Calming Breaths. Close your eyes if you like, and imagine a peaceful light or a calming crystal deep inside your own body – maybe in your chest, your heart, or your tummy. What color is it? What does it feel like? How does it make your nervous system feel settled? This is your internal guide helping you make a **choice** for calm."
    - "On your 'My Core Calm Crystal/Light' page, draw this 'core calm' or 'peace crystal' inside your body. You can draw yourself and where you feel it. What symbols or words help you remember to connect with this calm place and make that **choice**?"
    - "Remember, you can always connect to this core calm when your 'volcano' starts to rumble or your 'pressure' builds, helping your nervous system regulate through your **choice** to pause and connect."
  - **Facilitator Tips:** Guide with a gentle, calming voice. Emphasize that this is an internal resource they always carry, and that accessing it is a conscious

choice that empowers them, particularly after a pause. Validate all forms of "core calm." In this context, validate is the equivalent of acknowledging.

Chapter 4: The Weeping Willow and the Whispers of Sorrow

- **Core Emotional Theme(s):** Processing Sadness; Shifting Thought Patterns; Cultivating Gratitude and Joy.
- **Book Synopsis:** AJ and Whimsy arrive at the Planet of Sadness, shrouded in gray clouds and home to the drooping Pluvia who carry a deep sense of sorrow. Here, the Weeping Willow absorbs sadness and "Whispers of Sorrow" try to deepen despair. Recalling his mom's teachings, AJ shows the Pluvia how to release sad thoughts by imagining them floating away in bubbles and how to consciously choose joyful or grateful thoughts instead. Inspired, they create a "Symphony of Hope" through song, bringing light back to the planet and brightening Cordium.
- **Key Regulation & Wellness Concepts Introduced:**
  - Normalizing sadness as a valid emotion and understanding its physical sensations.
  - The concept that thoughts are not always facts, and we have a **choice** to engage with or release unhelpful thoughts ("thought diffusion").
  - Practicing cognitive shifting: intentionally choosing to focus on positive, joyful, or grateful thoughts to influence mood and nervous system state.
  - The power of creative expression (like music) and connection with others in processing and lifting sadness.
  - The ripple effect of shared joy and gratitude on personal and collective well-being.

Discussion Questions

For Young Explorers (Grades K-2):

- Before Reading: "What does it feel like in your body when you feel sad? Does it feel heavy, or quiet, or like tears? Where do you notice it?"
- After Reading: "What did the Pluvia look like, and how did they act on the Planet of Sadness? What were the 'Whispers of Sorrow' trying to make them feel?"
- After Reading: "AJ taught the Pluvia a trick with bubbles. What did they put in the bubbles, and where did the bubbles go? How did that help?"
- After Reading: "What did AJ ask the Pluvia to think about after the sad thoughts floated away? What made the Weeping Willow and the Pluvia start to feel better?"

For Middle Navigators (Grades 3-5):

- Before Reading: "Have you ever had a sad thought that seemed to get 'stuck' in your head, making you feel even heavier or more down? What was that like? Do you feel like you have a **choice** about how long that thought stays 'stuck'?"
- After Reading: "The Weeping Willow absorbed the Pluvia's sadness. How do our own bodies sometimes absorb sadness or stress? What happens when it's just 'absorbed' versus being processed and released through a **choice**?"
- After Reading: "AJ taught the Pluvia to imagine putting sad thoughts in bubbles and then choose to focus on joyful thoughts. How does having the **choice** to shift your thoughts help regulate your nervous system when you're feeling sad?"
- After Reading: "The Pluvia started to sing songs of hope and gratitude. How can creative expression or finding things to be grateful for help to change our mood and influence our nervous system, even when we're sad? What **choice** can we make to bring more 'music' into our lives?"

Staged Activities for Each Age Group

A. Young Explorers (Grades K-2)

1. **Activity: My Sadness Cloud (Absorb)**
   - **Objective(s):** To help children acknowledge and visually represent sadness, understanding that it can feel heavy like a cloud before learning ways to brighten it.
   - **Materials:** Paper, blue/gray/purple crayons or markers.
   - **Instructions:**
     - "On the Planet of Sadness, everything was covered in a veil of gray clouds. Sometimes, sadness can feel like a heavy cloud hovering over us or inside our body."
     - "On your paper, draw a big cloud. Inside or around the cloud, draw or color what your sadness cloud looks like or feels like. Is it dark? Does it make your shoulders droop? Does it make your eyes feel like rain?"
     - "After you draw your cloud, talk about how you feel it in your body. We notice our sadness so we can choose ways to help it feel lighter."
   - **Facilitator Tips:** Reiterate that sadness is a normal feeling. Validate their drawings and feelings without judgment. This is a simple step in emotional recognition.
   - **Printable Page Reference:** "My Sadness Cloud Drawing Page."

2. **Activity: Bubble Away Sad Thoughts (Do)**
   - **Objective(s):** To practice a playful, visual technique for detaching from and releasing unhelpful sad thoughts, fostering nervous system regulation through symbolic action and conscious **choice**.
   - **Materials:** Optional: a bottle of real bubbles and wand for demonstration; otherwise, just imagination.
   - **Instructions:**
     - "AJ taught the Pluvia a special trick: putting sad thoughts in bubbles and watching them float away. We have a **choice** about what we do with our thoughts – we don't have to keep every single one!"
     - "Think of a sad thought you might have. Now, imagine holding a giant bubble wand. Pretend to put that sad thought right into a bubble."
     - "Now, take a big breath (like our Cosmic Calming Breath) and gently blow that bubble away, watching it float up, up, and away until it disappears. The sad thought is gone, just like the bubble!"
     - Repeat 2-3 times. "Notice how your body feels a little lighter or calmer when you choose to let those thoughts go."
   - **Facilitator Tips:** Model the action clearly. Emphasize the *choice* to let the thought go. For very young children, focus more on the "blowing away" aspect.
   - **Printable Page Reference:** "Bubble Away My Sad Thoughts."
3. **Activity: My Grateful Rainbow (Connect)**
   - **Objective(s):** To practice intentionally shifting focus towards positive and grateful thoughts, influencing mood and nervous system state, reinforcing the **choice** to cultivate joy.
   - **Materials:** Paper, crayons/colored pencils/markers for rainbow colors.
   - **Instructions:**
     - "After the sad thoughts floated away, AJ told the Pluvia to think about joyful and peaceful things. That's like making a rainbow appear after the rain! We have a **choice** to look for the bright colors in our lives."
     - "Draw a big rainbow on your paper. In each color stripe, draw or write one thing that makes you feel happy, calm, or grateful. (Give examples: my pet, a favorite food, playing outside, a hug, my family)."
     - "As you draw each one, take a few Cosmic Calming Breaths. Notice how focusing on these positive things can make your body feel warmer, calmer, and more joyful. This is your **choice** to bring more light into your inner world."

        - Optional: Share one item from their tree.
    - **Facilitator Tips:** Encourage specific examples rather than general statements. Help children identify even small things to be grateful for. Connect the positive feeling to a regulated nervous system.
    - **Printable Page Reference:** "My Grateful Rainbow."

B. Middle Navigators (Grades 3-5)

1. **Activity: The Sorrowful Sound Check (Absorb)**
    - **Objective(s):** To help students differentiate between unhelpful, repetitive "whispers of sorrow" and more constructive thoughts, recognizing their impact on emotional and physical well-being. This reinforces the **choice** in internal dialogue.
    - **Materials:** Whiteboard/chart paper, markers.
    - **Instructions:**
        - "The Planet of Sadness had 'Whispers of Sorrow' that fed on hopelessness. Our minds can sometimes play these 'whispers' on repeat, making us feel more sad or stuck."
        - "Let's make two columns on the board/paper: 'Whispers of Sorrow' and 'Sounds of Hope.' In the first column, brainstorm some common 'whispers of sorrow' (e.g., 'I can't do it,' 'Nobody cares,' 'It's too hard,' 'I always mess up')."
        - "Now, how does listening to those 'whispers' make your body feel? (e.g., heavy, slumped, tired, tight chest). This is your nervous system reacting to those thoughts. Does listening to them feel like a helpful **choice**?"
        - "In the 'Sounds of Hope' column, brainstorm what a compassionate inner voice might say instead (e.g., 'I can try my best,' 'My friends care,' 'I can ask for help,' 'Mistakes help me learn'). How does *that* feel in your body? Which voice do you **choose** to listen to?"
    - **Facilitator Tips:** Emphasize that these are just *thoughts* and we have a **choice** which ones to amplify. Connect the internal dialogue to nervous system activation (feeling heavy vs. feeling lighter).
    - **Printable Page Reference:** "Whispers of Sorrow vs. Sounds of Hope."

2. **Activity: My Thought Bubble Release (Do)**
   - **Objective(s):** To actively practice the technique of externalizing and releasing unhelpful sad thoughts, empowering students with a conscious **choice** for thought management and nervous system regulation.
   - **Materials:** Paper, pens/pencils, (Optional: actual clear balloons or a clear plastic bag).
   - **Instructions:**
     - "AJ taught the Pluvia to put sad thoughts into bubbles and watch them float away. This helps us practice that we have a **choice** about whether we carry every thought with us, or if we can let some go."
     - "On your paper (or into your imaginary balloon/bag), quickly write down a sad or unhelpful thought you might have (it can be general, not personal if they prefer). Don't censor it, just get it out."
     - "Now, imagine crumpling that paper into a tiny ball, or tying off the balloon. As you do, really imagine that thought is now contained, no longer bouncing around in your head."
     - "Take a Cosmic Calming Breath. Now, on the count of three, we're going to let that thought go. You can toss the paper ball gently into a bin, or imagine the balloon floating away. On 3... 1, 2, 3, let it go!"
     - "Notice how your body feels now that you've consciously made the **choice** to release that thought. Did your nervous system feel a little lighter?"
   - **Facilitator Tips:** Ensure a safe and respectful environment for expressing thoughts. Emphasize the *choice* to release the thought, not necessarily making it disappear forever, but reducing its immediate impact. If using real objects, ensure proper disposal.
   - **Printable Page Reference:** "My Thought Bubble Page."
3. **Activity: My Gratitude Tree (Connect)**
   - **Objective(s):** To cultivate a practice of focusing on gratitude, which positively impacts mood, shifts perspective, and helps regulate the nervous system towards a more joyful state. This reinforces the **choice** to cultivate joy.
   - **Materials:** Paper, crayons/colored pencils/markers.
   - **Instructions:**
     - "After letting sad thoughts go, AJ encouraged the Pluvia to focus on things that bring joy and gratitude, helping their nervous systems feel lighter. Gratitude is like sunshine for our inner tree!"

        - "On your 'My Gratitude Tree' page, you'll see a tree. On each leaf or branch, draw or write something specific you are grateful for. It could be something big (family) or small (a cozy blanket, a favorite snack, a sunny day, a good song)."
        - "As you fill your tree, take a few Cosmic Calming Breaths. Notice how focusing on these positive things can make your body feel warmer, calmer, and more joyful. This is your **choice** to bring more light into your inner world."
        - Optional: Share one item from their tree.
    - **Facilitator Tips:** Encourage specific examples rather than general statements. Emphasize that practicing gratitude is a conscious **choice** that can retrain the brain and influence the nervous system over time.
    - **Printable Page Reference:** "My Gratitude Tree."

Chapter 5: The Starlight Singers and the Symphony of Hope

- **Core Emotional Theme(s):** Overcoming Doubt & Exhaustion; Cultivating Self-Compassion & Hope; Recognizing the Power of Community Connection.
- **Book Synopsis:** After helping creatures across the universe, AJ feels a twinge of doubt and exhaustion. His spaceship is drawn to a brilliant light, leading him to the ethereal Starlight Singers. They remind AJ that he is not alone, and through their harmonious songs of courage, peace, and joy, they reinforce the power of hope, faith, and community. AJ's spirits are lifted, and he finds renewed determination to complete his mission.
- **Key Regulation & Wellness Concepts Introduced:**
    - Recognizing and addressing feelings of doubt or overwhelm as part of any journey.
    - Practicing self-compassion and gentle self-talk when feeling tired or unsure.
    - Understanding the regulating power of connection and community on the nervous system.
    - Cultivating hope as an internal resource for resilience and perseverance.
    - The universal language of creative expression (like music) for healing and connection.

Discussion Questions

For Young Explorers (Grades K-2):

- Before Reading: "Have you ever felt tired or a little unsure, even after working really hard on something? How does that feeling make your body feel?"
- After Reading: "What were the Starlight Singers like? What did their voices make AJ feel?"
- After Reading: "The Singers told AJ he was not alone. Who are some people in your life who help you when you feel tired or unsure?"
- After Reading: "The Singers sang about courage, peace, and joy. How can listening to happy music or being with friends make your body feel better and more energetic?"

For Middle Navigators (Grades 3-5):

- Before Reading: "Even when we've achieved a lot, sometimes doubt or exhaustion can creep in. When you've felt that way, what kind of thoughts 'whisper' to you?"

- After Reading: "AJ questioned if he was strong enough. How did the Starlight Singers help him overcome his doubts? What was their main message?"
- After Reading: "The Singers used music to help AJ. How can listening to, or making, music regulate our nervous system and shift our mood? What's your 'symphony of hope'?"
- After Reading: "The Singers sang about the creatures AJ had helped. How did remembering his connections and positive impact help AJ find renewed purpose and energy? How does connecting with your community regulate your nervous system?"

Staged Activities for Each Age Group

A. Young Explorers (Grades K-2)

1. **Activity: My Doubt Cloud (Absorb)**
    - **Objective(s):** To acknowledge and externalize feelings of doubt or being overwhelmed, understanding that these are temporary feelings.
    - **Materials:** Paper, gray/light blue crayons or markers.
    - **Instructions:**
        - "After helping so many planets, AJ felt a little tired and unsure, like a little cloud of doubt was floating over him. It's okay to feel doubt sometimes."
        - "On your paper, draw a 'doubt cloud.' What does your doubt cloud look like? Does it feel heavy? Does it make you want to be quiet?"
        - "We notice our doubt, but we don't let it stay forever. Just like clouds can pass, our doubts can too, especially when we remember our inner sparkle!"
    - **Facilitator Tips:** Emphasize that doubt is a normal feeling. Validate their feelings. This helps children recognize inner states.
    - **Printable Page Reference:** "My Doubt Cloud Visual."
2. **Activity: Light My Sparkle Affirmations (Do)**
    - **Objective(s):** To practice positive self-talk and affirmations to counter feelings of doubt, strengthening self-compassion and promoting a regulated nervous system.
    - **Materials:** Pre-cut paper star shapes (or students cut their own), markers/crayons.
    - **Instructions:**

        - "When AJ felt doubtful, the Starlight Singers reminded him of his strength and that he wasn't alone. We can remind ourselves how amazing we are! That's called an 'affirmation' – a kind and true message to yourself."
        - "On your star, write or draw one thing that makes *you* amazing, brave, or kind. (Examples: 'I am strong,' 'I am kind,' 'I can try,' 'I am loved')."
        - "Now, hold your star. Take a Cosmic Calming Breath. Say your affirmation quietly or out loud. Feel that warmth of your inner sparkle shining brightly, helping your body feel calm and strong."
        - Display stars to create a "Constellation of Strengths."
    - **Facilitator Tips:** Guide children to focus on qualities rather than external achievements. Encourage genuine self-compassion. This practice helps to shift the nervous system towards a positive state.
    - **Printable Page Reference:** "Sparkle Affirmation Stars."
3. **Activity: Our Community Constellation (Connect)**
    - **Objective(s):** To help children visualize and appreciate their support network (family, friends, teachers) as a source of strength and comfort, reinforcing connection and safety for the nervous system.
    - **Materials:** Large sheet of dark blue or black paper, glow-in-the-dark stars or white/yellow star stickers, markers.
    - **Instructions:**
        - "The Starlight Singers reminded AJ that he was part of a bigger community, and he was never truly alone. Just like stars make a constellation, the people who love and support us make our own special 'Community Constellation.'"
        - "On our big paper, let's create our 'Community Constellation.' Each star sticker or drawn star will represent someone who helps you, loves you, or makes you feel safe. Write their name on it, or draw a symbol for them."
        - "Place your star on our big paper. See how all our stars together make a bright, supportive constellation! How does it feel in your body to know you are connected?"
    - **Facilitator Tips:** Emphasize the feeling of safety and belonging. Encourage children to think broadly about their support network (teachers, family, friends, pets).
    - **Printable Page Reference:** "Our Community Constellation Map."

B. Middle Navigators (Grades 3-5)

1. **Activity: The Weight of My Worries (Absorb)**
    - **Objective(s):** To help students recognize and externalize feelings of doubt, overwhelm, or exhaustion, and how these can feel heavy, impacting their nervous system.
    - **Materials:** Small slips of paper, pencils, a small bucket or "worry jar," a balance scale (optional).
    - **Instructions:**
        - "Even after doing so much good, AJ felt a 'twinge of doubt' and exhaustion. Sometimes, our worries or doubts can feel heavy, like a weight we're carrying, making our nervous system feel heavy too."
        - "On these small slips of paper, write down one worry, doubt, or something that feels heavy right now. It can be general, or something specific. (Emphasize privacy: they don't have to share what they wrote)."
        - "Now, one by one, crumple your paper into a tiny ball. Feel its weight. Now, place it in our 'Worry Jar' (or on one side of a balance scale). Notice how many worries we have as a group, and how they add up."
        - "Discussion: 'How does it feel in your body to carry these worries? Does seeing them together make you feel lighter or heavier? How does our nervous system feel when we have many worries weighing us down?'"
    - **Facilitator Tips:** Maintain a safe, non-judgmental space. Stress that this is for *identifying* feelings, not dwelling on them. Transition quickly to the next activity of releasing.
    - **Printable Page Reference:** "Worry Weight Slips & Jar Label."
2. **Activity: Symphony of Strengths (Do)**
    - **Objective(s):** To actively identify and acknowledge personal strengths and positive qualities, boosting self-compassion and activating a positive nervous system state.
    - **Materials:** Paper, markers/crayons, (Optional: calm, uplifting instrumental music).
    - **Instructions:**
        - "The Starlight Singers created a 'Symphony of Hope' by singing about courage, peace, and joy. We can create our own 'Symphony of Strengths' by focusing on what makes us strong, capable, and amazing!"

        - "On your 'Symphony of Strengths' page (which has musical notes or staff), write or draw things you are good at, qualities you have, or times you've been brave or kind. (Examples: I am a good listener, I am creative, I am resilient, I am helpful, I can solve problems, I am a good friend)."
        - "As you write or draw each strength, take a Cosmic Calming Breath. Feel the positive energy of these thoughts filling your body. This helps your nervous system feel strong and hopeful."
        - Optional: Share one strength aloud, contributing to a "group symphony."
    - **Facilitator Tips:** Encourage specific examples. Reiterate that everyone has unique strengths. This activity focuses on building internal resources and positive self-perception.
    - **Printable Page Reference:** "My Symphony of Strengths."
3. **Activity: My Support Constellation (Connect)**
    - **Objective(s):** To help students recognize and appreciate their personal support network, understanding that connection provides comfort and resilience, regulating their nervous system through a sense of belonging.
    - **Materials:** Paper, markers/crayons, optional: yarn/string to connect stars.
    - **Instructions:**
        - "The Starlight Singers reminded AJ that he was never alone, surrounded by a community of support. We all have people in our lives who shine for us, like stars in our own 'Support Constellation.'"
        - "On your 'My Support Constellation Map' page, draw a large circle in the middle and write your name. Then, draw stars around it. In each star, write or draw someone (or even a pet!) who supports you, helps you feel safe, listens to you, or makes you feel good. (Examples: family members, friends, teachers, counselors, coaches, neighbors)."
        - "If you like, draw lines connecting your central star to your support stars. Take a Cosmic Calming Breath. Notice how drawing these connections makes your body feel safe and cared for. This sense of connection regulates our nervous system."
        - Optional: Share one star from their constellation.
    - **Facilitator Tips:** Encourage thinking broadly about support. Emphasize that seeking help and relying on others is a strength. Highlight the feeling of safety that comes from knowing you're connected.

- **Printable Page Reference:** "My Support Constellation Map."

Chapter 6: Return to Cordium and the Kindness Ripple Effect

- **Core Emotional Theme(s):** The Enduring Power of Kindness; Sustaining Personal Well-being & Growth; The Ripple Effect of Compassionate Action.
- **Book Synopsis:** AJ returns to a fully re-brightened Cordium, meeting Caritas, the constellation's guardian. She affirms that AJ's kindness created a powerful ripple effect across the universe, showing him images of the thriving Worrions, Flamma, and Pluvia. Caritas gifts AJ with a "Seed of Kindness" to plant on Earth, reminding him that his journey of spreading kindness and self-care is just beginning, culminating in the powerful message: "You are amazing. Take care of YOU!"
- **Key Regulation & Wellness Concepts Introduced:**
    - Understanding the broad and lasting impact of individual acts of kindness on others and the environment (the "ripple effect").
    - Reinforcing the importance of ongoing self-care and nervous system regulation as a continuous practice for holistic health.
    - Integrating and celebrating learned skills as tools for lifelong well-being and resilience.
    - Cultivating self-compassion and recognizing one's inherent worth ("You are amazing. Take care of YOU!").
    - The concept of contributing to a larger community and world through personal growth and conscious **choice**.

Discussion Questions

For Young Explorers (Grades K-2):

- Before Reading: "What are some ways we can show kindness to people, animals, or even our planet?"
- After Reading: "What did Caritas tell AJ about kindness? What does 'ripple effect' mean?"
- After Reading: "AJ got a special 'Seed of Kindness' to plant on Earth. What do you think that seed might grow into, and what would it help people remember?"
- After Reading: "The book reminds us: 'You are amazing. Take care of YOU!' What does 'take care of YOU' mean for your body and your feelings?"

For Middle Navigators (Grades 3-5):

- Before Reading: "Think about a time someone was kind to you. How did that make you feel? Did it change your day or how you treated someone else?"
- After Reading: "Caritas shows AJ how his kindness changed the Worrions, Flamma, and Pluvia. How does one person's compassionate actions create a 'ripple effect' that spreads far beyond them?"
- After Reading: "The message 'You are amazing. Take care of YOU!' is very important. Why is practicing self-care and self-compassion just as important as being kind to others for maintaining a regulated nervous system?"
- After Reading: "AJ's journey wasn't over, it was 'just beginning.' What does that tell us about practicing emotional regulation and kindness in our lives? Why is it something we keep practicing?"

Staged Activities for Each Age Group

A. Young Explorers (Grades K-2)

1. **Activity: My Kindness Ripple (Absorb)**
   - **Objective(s):** To visually represent how small acts of kindness can spread outwards and positively affect others.
   - **Materials:** Paper, crayons/markers.
   - **Instructions:**
     - "Caritas taught AJ that kindness creates a 'ripple effect.' When you throw a pebble in water, the ripples spread out. Kindness is like that pebble!"
     - "On your paper, draw a small circle in the middle and write 'Me' or draw your face. Now, draw bigger and bigger circles or 'ripples' around it."
     - "In the first ripple, draw or write one kind thing you can do. In the next ripple, draw how that kindness might spread to a friend or family member. In the outer ripples, draw how it might spread even further, to your school or community! See how your kindness grows!"
   - **Facilitator Tips:** Emphasize that even small acts create big ripples. Connect the visual to the feeling of warmth and connection.
   - **Printable Page Reference:** "My Kindness Ripple Drawing Page."
2. **Activity: You Are Amazing! Mirror Message (Do)**
   - **Objective(s):** To practice positive self-talk and self-compassion, reinforcing the message "You are amazing. Take care of YOU!"

- **Materials:** Cardstock or thick paper cut into a simple mirror shape, markers/crayons, optional: shiny foil or reflective paper.
- **Instructions:**
  - "AJ got a special message from his mom: 'You are amazing. Take care of YOU!' This is a message for all of us. Taking care of ourselves helps our nervous system stay regulated."
  - "On your paper 'mirror,' write or draw one thing that makes *you* amazing. It could be a quality you have, something you do well, or something you love about yourself."
  - "Now, hold your 'mirror' up to yourself. Look into it and say your amazing message quietly or out loud. Take a Cosmic Calming Breath. Feel how good it feels to be kind to yourself."
- **Facilitator Tips:** Encourage genuine self-reflection. Explain that self-compassion is a powerful tool for well-being.
- **Printable Page Reference:** "You Are Amazing! Mirror Message Template."

3. **Activity: My Seed of Kindness Pledge (Connect)**
   - **Objective(s):** To commit to an ongoing practice of kindness and self-care, symbolizing future growth and contribution to holistic well-being.
   - **Materials:** Paper, crayons/markers. Optional: actual seeds for planting (if feasible and safe).
   - **Instructions:**
     - "Caritas gave AJ a 'Seed of Kindness' to plant on Earth, symbolizing his continued journey. We can all plant a 'Seed of Kindness' by making a promise to keep growing in kindness and taking care of ourselves."
     - "On your 'My Seed of Kindness Pledge' page, draw a large seed or a small plant in a pot. Inside or around it, write or draw one promise you will make for the coming days or weeks. This could be: 'I will say kind words,' 'I will help a friend,' 'I will take 3 deep breaths when I'm mad,' or 'I will play outside every day.'"
     - "This is your promise to keep your own inner sparkle shining and to help kindness grow in the world!"
   - **Facilitator Tips:** Encourage realistic and actionable pledges. Discuss how consistent practice helps these "seeds" grow.
   - **Printable Page Reference:** "My Seed of Kindness Pledge."

B. Middle Navigators (Grades 3-5)

1. **Activity: My Kindness Ripple Effect Map (Absorb)**
    - **Objective(s):** To visualize and articulate how individual acts of kindness create a broad and lasting positive impact on various spheres of influence.
    - **Materials:** Paper, markers/pens.
    - **Instructions:**
        - "Caritas explained that kindness is a powerful 'ripple effect' that spreads. We can map out how our own kindness can create these ripples."
        - "On your 'My Kindness Ripple Effect Map' page, write 'Me' in the central circle. In the first ring, write or draw ways your kindness affects your closest circle (Family, Best Friends). In the next ring, consider how it reaches your broader connections (Classmates, Neighbors, Teachers). In the outermost ring, how might your kindness ripple out to your Community or even the World?"
        - "Think about how each kind choice activates positive feelings in your nervous system and helps those around you feel more regulated, creating a wave of compassion."
    - **Facilitator Tips:** Encourage specific examples for each ring. Highlight the interconnectedness and the feeling of contributing positively.
    - **Printable Page Reference:** "My Kindness Ripple Effect Map."
2. **Activity: My Self-Care Blueprint (Do)**
    - **Objective(s):** To help students create a personalized plan for consistent self-care and nervous system regulation, integrating the skills learned throughout the book.
    - **Materials:** Paper, markers/crayons.
    - **Instructions:**
        - "The message 'Take care of YOU!' is vital. Just like a builder uses a blueprint, we can create a 'Self-Care Blueprint' for our own well-being, mapping out how we keep our body and mind regulated."
        - "On your 'My Self-Care Blueprint' page (which might look like a house, a ship, or a tree), you'll see different sections. In each section, draw or write specific ways you will practice self-care and regulation. (Examples: 'Cosmic Calming Breath,' '5-4-3-2-1,' 'Playing outside,'

'Reading,' 'Getting enough sleep,' 'Spending time with family/friends,' 'Doing something creative')."
    - "This blueprint is your guide to building a strong, regulated inner self, preparing you to thrive."
  - **Facilitator Tips:** Encourage practical, realistic self-care ideas. Emphasize that self-care is a **choice** and a crucial component of long-term holistic health and resilience.
  - **Printable Page Reference:** "My Self-Care Blueprint."
3. **Activity: My Journey of Growth Constellation (Connect)**
  - **Objective(s):** To encourage reflection on personal growth and skill development throughout their journey with the book, fostering a sense of accomplishment and continued purpose.
  - **Materials:** Paper, markers/pens, optional: star stickers.
  - **Instructions:**
    - "AJ's journey didn't end when Cordium was bright again; it was just beginning. Your journey of growth and kindness is also ongoing!"
    - "On your 'My Journey of Growth Constellation Map' page, you'll see a path or a constellation. Mark a starting point ('My Beginning'). Then, along the path or at different stars, reflect on and write down:
      - One new skill you learned (e.g., 'Cosmic Calming Breath').
      - One way you learned to manage an emotion (e.g., 'Letting go of sad thoughts').
      - One way you connected with others or showed kindness.
      - How your body or nervous system feels more often now."
    - "At the end, mark 'My Ongoing Journey.' This map reminds you how much you've grown and how you can keep shining!"
  - **Facilitator Tips:** Encourage celebrating progress, no matter how small. Emphasize that practice is continuous. This activity promotes a growth mindset and reinforces the value of their efforts.
  - **Printable Page Reference:** "My Journey of Growth Constellation Map."

Printable Handouts Reference List

A Note on the Printables: The printable pages included in this workbook are designed to be a helpful starting point. They are intended as a tool to support the lessons and activities for both young explorers and middle navigators. You are welcome to use these printables as they are, or you can use them as inspiration to create your own versions that best suit your unique classroom, counseling session, or home environment. The goal is to provide a flexible and supportive guide that you can tailor to your own needs.

Chapter 1: The Night the Stars Went Dim

For Young Explorers (Grades K-2):

- **Printable:** "My Belly Buddy Breath Visual"
- **Printable:** "My Inner Sparkle Drawing Page"
- **Printable:** "Rainbow Breath & Body Anchor Visual"

For Middle Navigators (Grades 3-5):

- **Printable:** "Cosmic Calming Breath & Grounding Visual"
- **Printable:** "My Inner Guide Journal Page"

Chapter 2: Lost in the Whispering Woods

For Young Explorers (Grades K-2):

- **Printable:** "My Quiet Space Drawing Page"

For Middle Navigators (Grades 3-5):

- **Printable:** "My 5-4-3-2-1 Power Up Checklist"
- **Printable:** "My Sunshine Explorer Courage Shield Template"

Chapter 3: Destination: Planet of Anger

For Young Explorers (Grades K-2):

- **Printable:** "My Anger Volcano Drawing Page"
- **Printable:** "Cool-Down Breath Visual"

- **Printable:** "Calm Voice, Loud Voice Visual"

For Middle Navigators (Grades 3-5):

- **Printable:** "My Anger Thermometer & Warning Signs"
- **Printable:** "Calm Communication Scenario Cards"
- **Printable:** "My Core Calm Crystal/Light"

Chapter 4: The Weeping Willow and the Whispers of Sorrow

For Young Explorers (Grades K-2):

- **Printable:** "My Sadness Cloud Drawing Page"
- **Printable:** "Bubble Away My Sad Thoughts"
- **Printable:** "My Grateful Rainbow"

For Middle Navigators (Grades 3-5):

- **Printable:** "Whispers of Sorrow vs. Sounds of Hope"
- **Printable:** "My Thought Bubble Page"
- **Printable:** "My Gratitude Tree"

Chapter 5: The Starlight Singers and the Symphony of Hope

For Young Explorers (Grades K-2):

- **Printable:** "My Doubt Cloud Visual"
- **Printable:** "Sparkle Affirmation Stars"
- **Printable:** "Our Community Constellation Map"

For Middle Navigators (Grades 3-5):

- **Printable:** "Worry Weight Slips & Jar Label"
- **Printable:** "My Symphony of Strengths"
- **Printable:** "My Support Constellation Map"

Chapter 6: Return to Cordium and the Kindness Ripple Effect

For Young Explorers (Grades K-2):

- **Printable:** "My Kindness Ripples Drawing Page"

- **Printable:** "You Are Amazing! Mirror Message Template"
- **Printable:** "My Seed of Kindness Pledge"

For Middle Navigators (Grades 3-5):

- **Printable:** "My Kindness Ripples Effect Map"
- **Printable:** "My Self-Care Blueprint"
- **Printable:** "My Journey of Growth Constellation Map"

Bonus Worksheets:

- **Printable:** Coloring page choices
- **Printable:** “Young Explorers Kindness Constellation Word Search” (with answers)
- **Printable:** “Middle Navigators Kindness Constellation Word Search” (with answers)
- **Printable:** “You are amazing. Take care of YOU!” coloring sheet
- **Printable:** “The universe needs you. YOU are amazing!” coloring sheet

Appendix: All Printable Pages

MY BELLY BUDDY BREATH VISUAL

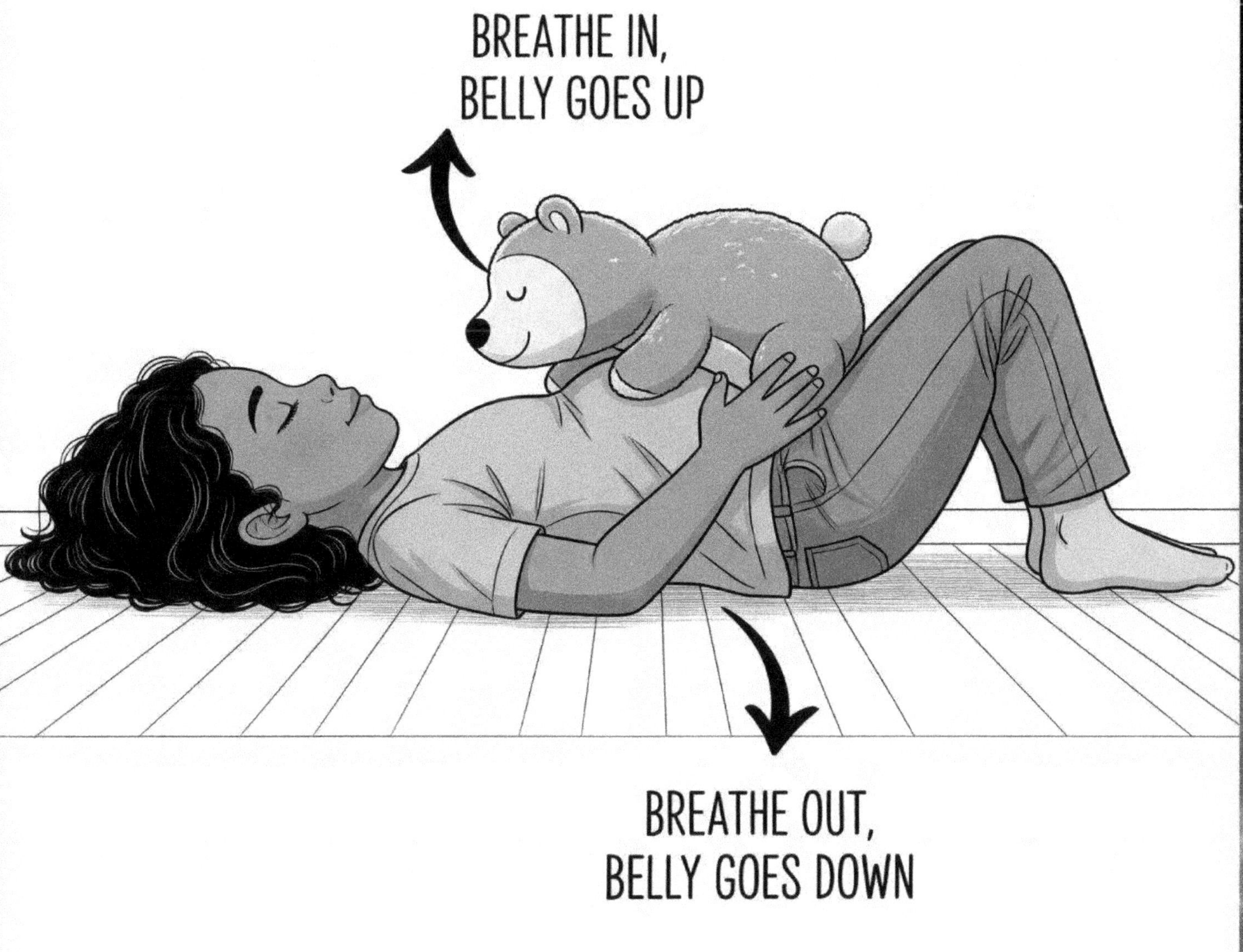

MY INNER SPARKLE

RAINBOW BREATH AND BODY ANCHOR VISUAL

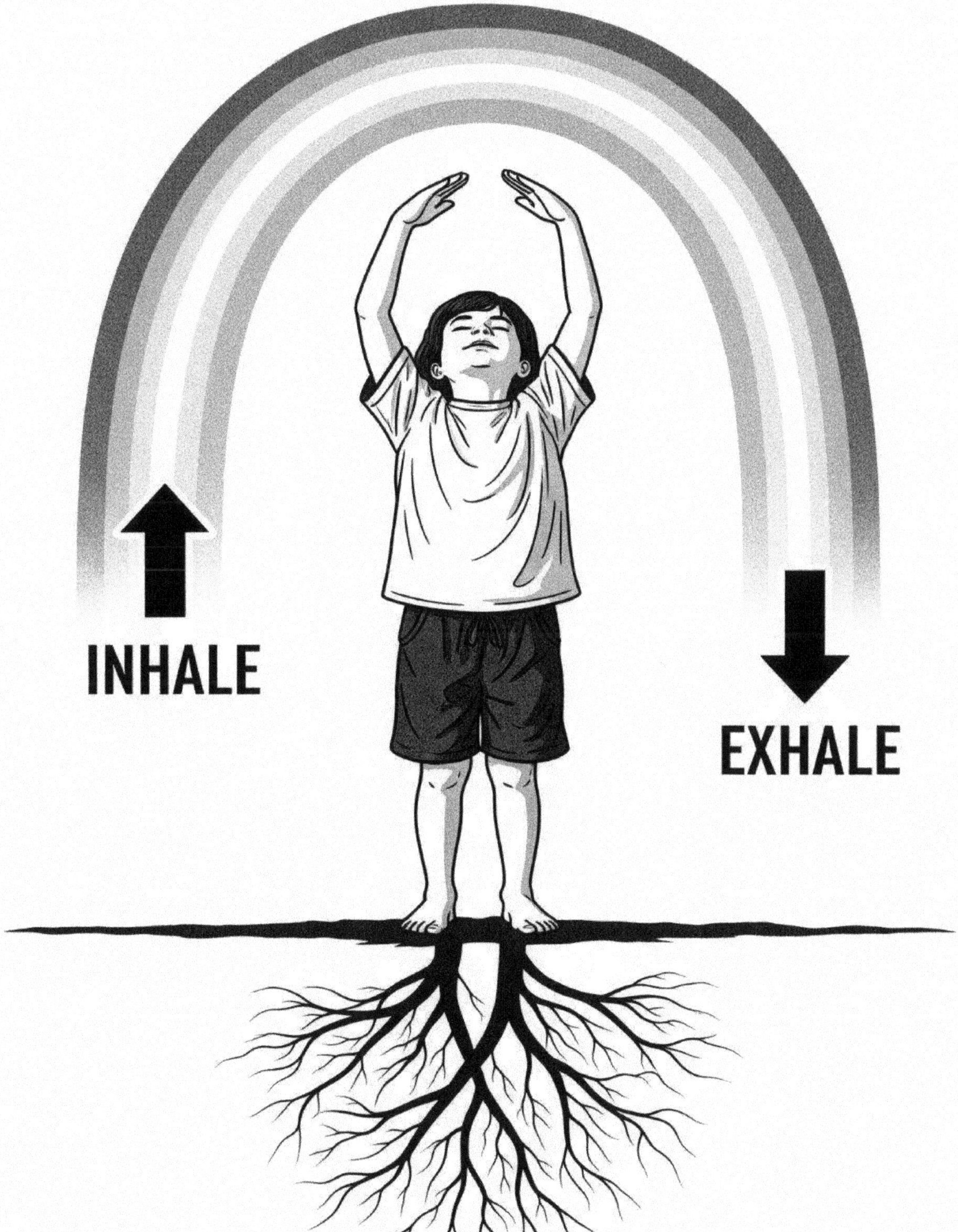

COSMIC CALMING BREATH AND GROUNDING VISUAL

MY INNER GUIDE

JOURNAL PAGE

What am I feeling?	What am I I thinking	What matters to me?

MY QUIET SPACE

MY 5-4-3-2-1 POWER UP CHECKLIST

Write or draw pictures of 5 things you can see, 4 things you can touch, 3 things you can hear, 2 things you can smell, and 1 thing you can taste.

THE SUNSHINE EXPLORER COURAGE SHIELD TEMPLATE

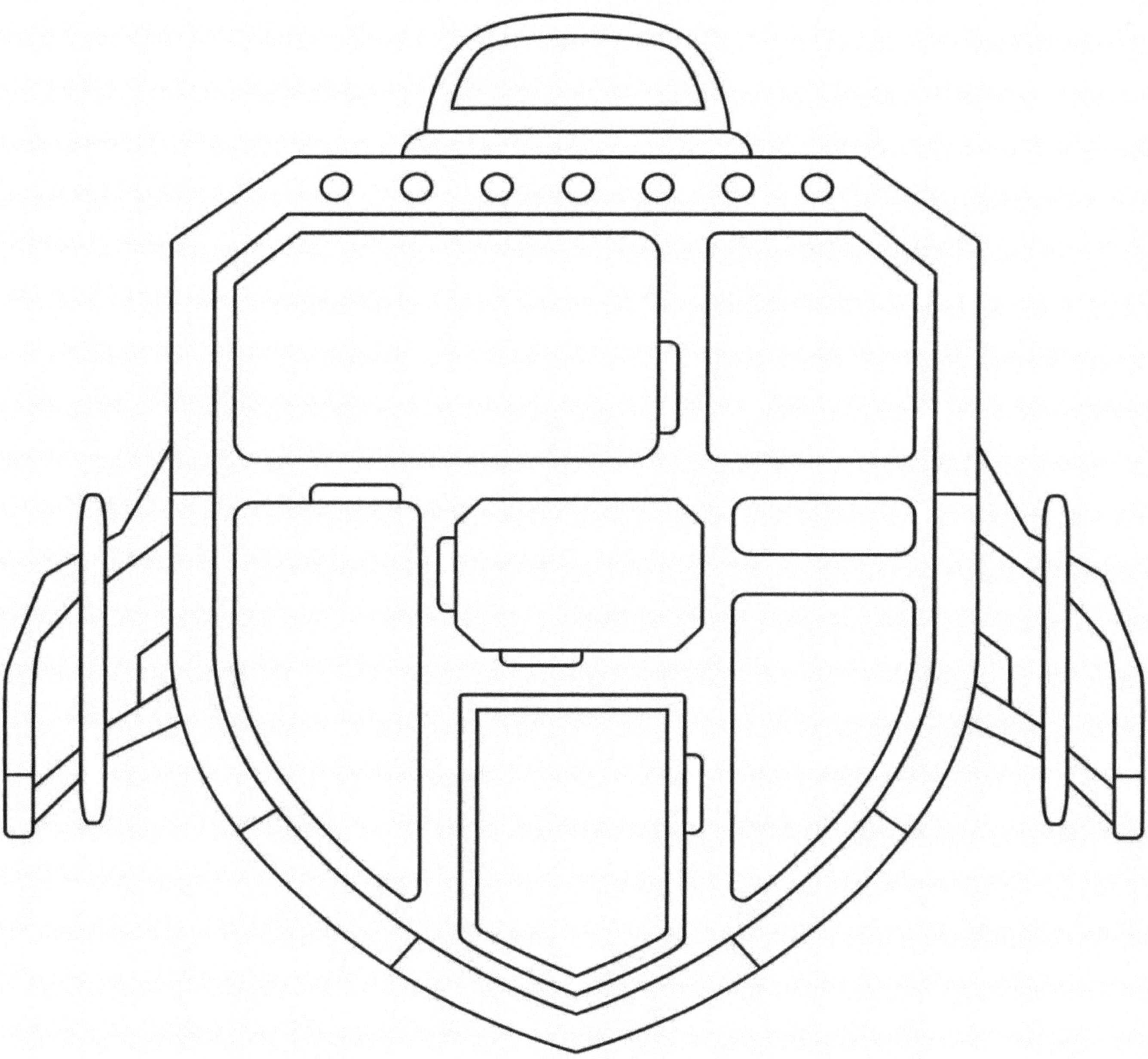

THE SUNSHINE EXPLORER COURAGE SHIELD TEMPLATE

MY ANGER VOLCANO

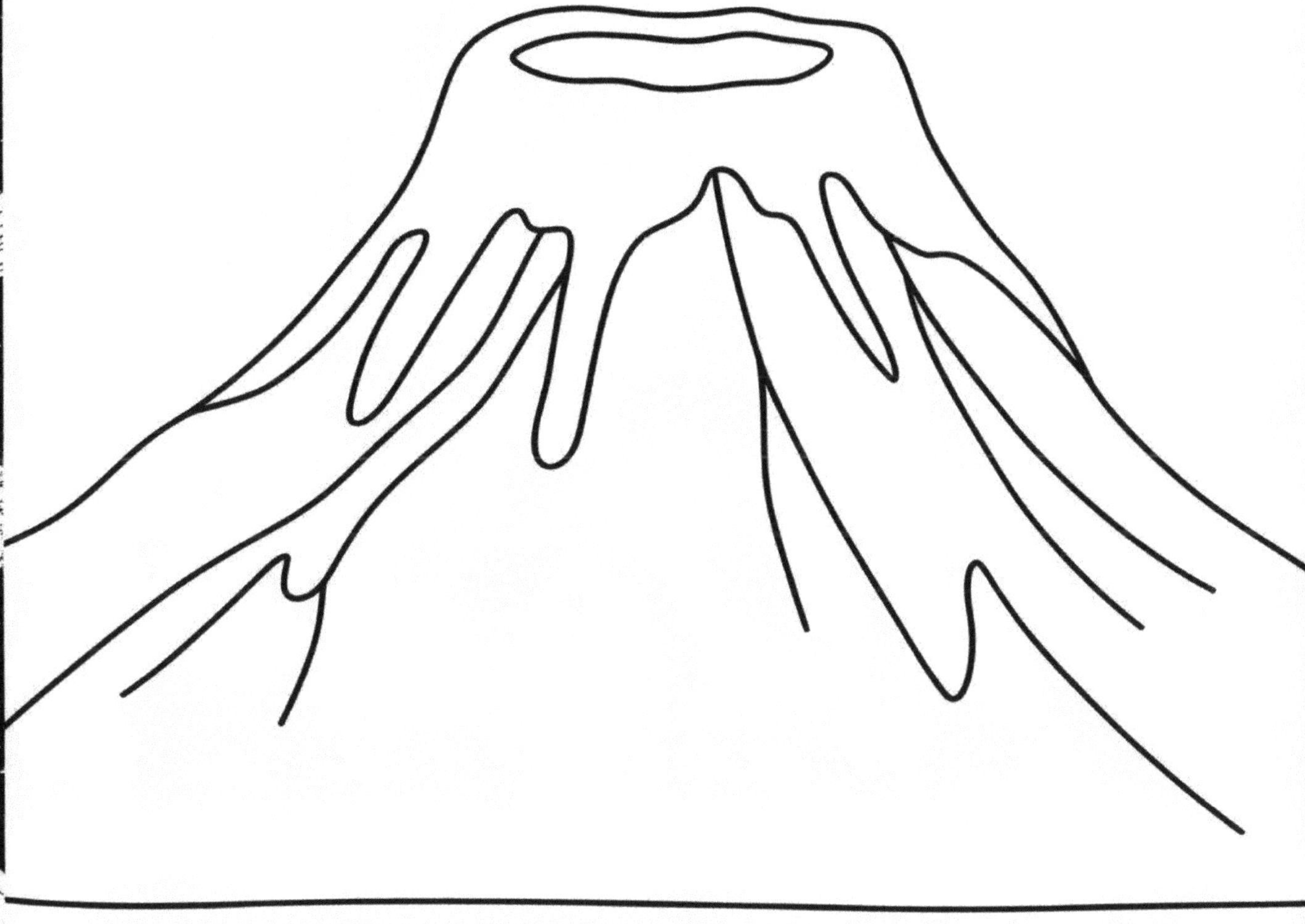

COOL DOWN BREATH VISUAL

Big breath in...and, big breath out.
...blow out your candle.

CALM VOICE, LOUD VOICE

LOUD VOICE

CALM VOICE

MY ANGER THERMOMETER

Focus on your body.

From your head to your toes, what do you feel? Where do you feel it?

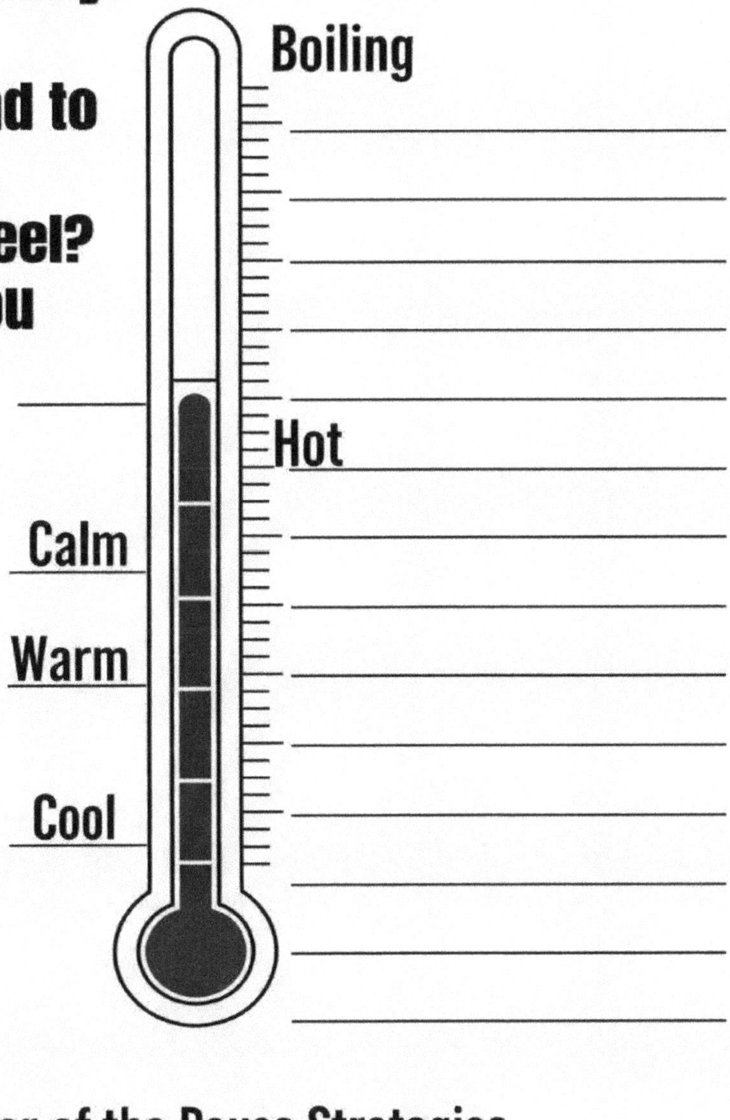

Power of the Pause Strategies

CALM COMMUNICATION SCENARIO CARDS

Fill in each card with a relatable scenario that might trigger anger or frustration, and prompt discussion for healthy ways to communicate in these scenarios.

MY CORE CALM CRYSTAL/LIGHT

MY CORE CALM

CRYSTAL/LIGHT

MY SADNESS CLOUD DRAWING PAGE

BUBBLE AWAY MY SAD THOUGHTS

MY GRATEFUL RAINBOW

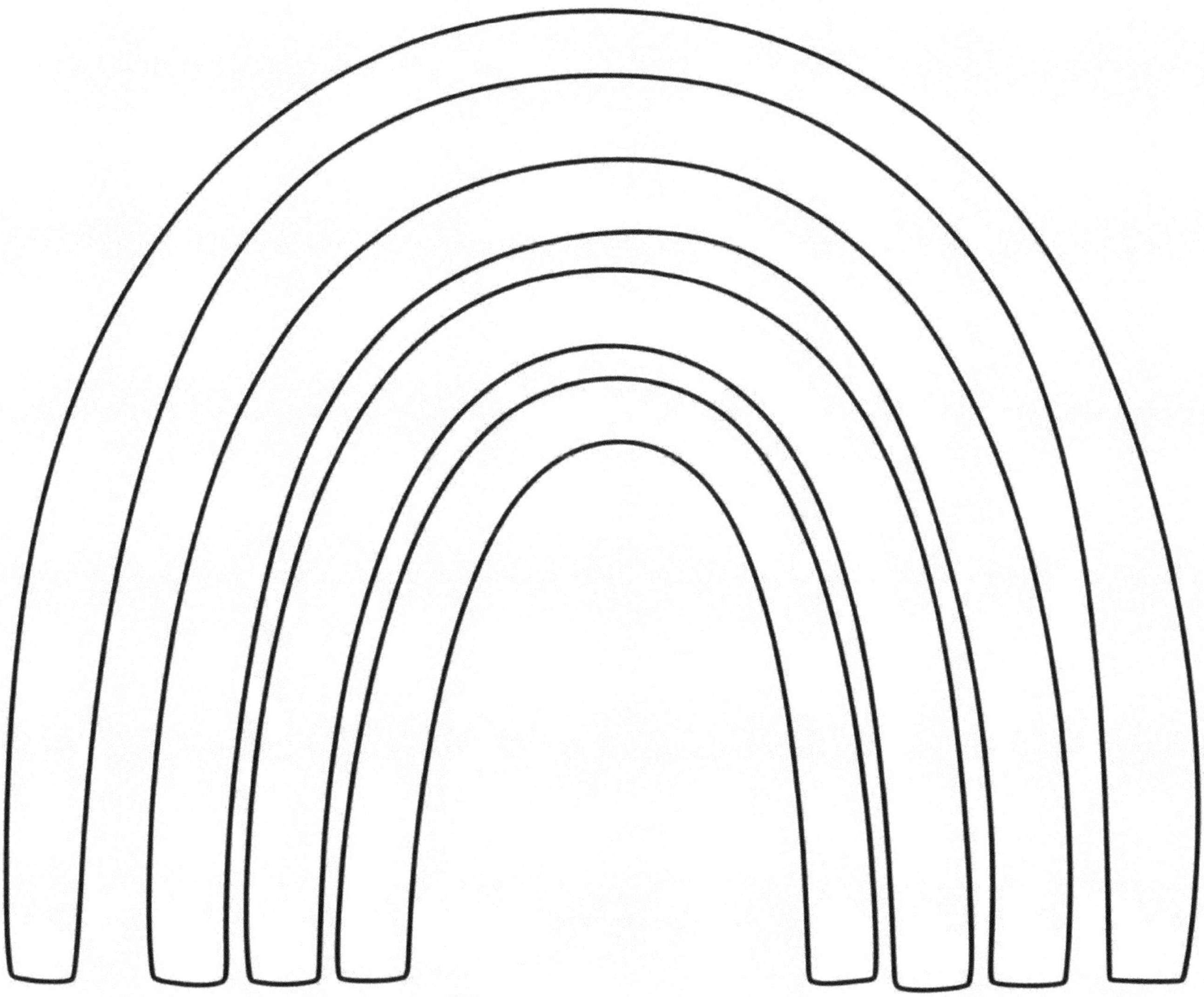

WHISPERS OF SORROW vs SOUNDS OF HOPE

WHISPERS OF SORROW	SOUNDS OF HOPE

MY THOUGHT BUBBLE PAGE

MY GRATITUDE TREE

MY DOUBT CLOUD

SPARKLE AFFIRMATION STARS

OUR COMMUNITY CONSTELLATION MAP

WORRY WEIGHT SLIPS, AND JAR LABELS

MY SYMPHONY OF STRENGTHS

MY SUPPORT CONSTELLATION MAP

MY KINDNESS RIPPLES DRAWING PAGE

YOU ARE AMAZING MIRROR

MY SEED OF KINDNESS PLEDGE

MY KINDNESS RIPPLES EFFECT MAP

MY SELF-CARE BLUEPRINT

Write or draw self-care and regulation practices that you can take with you daily on your journey. What will you need on your Sunshine Explorer?!

MY JOURNEY OF GROWTH CONSTELLATION MAP

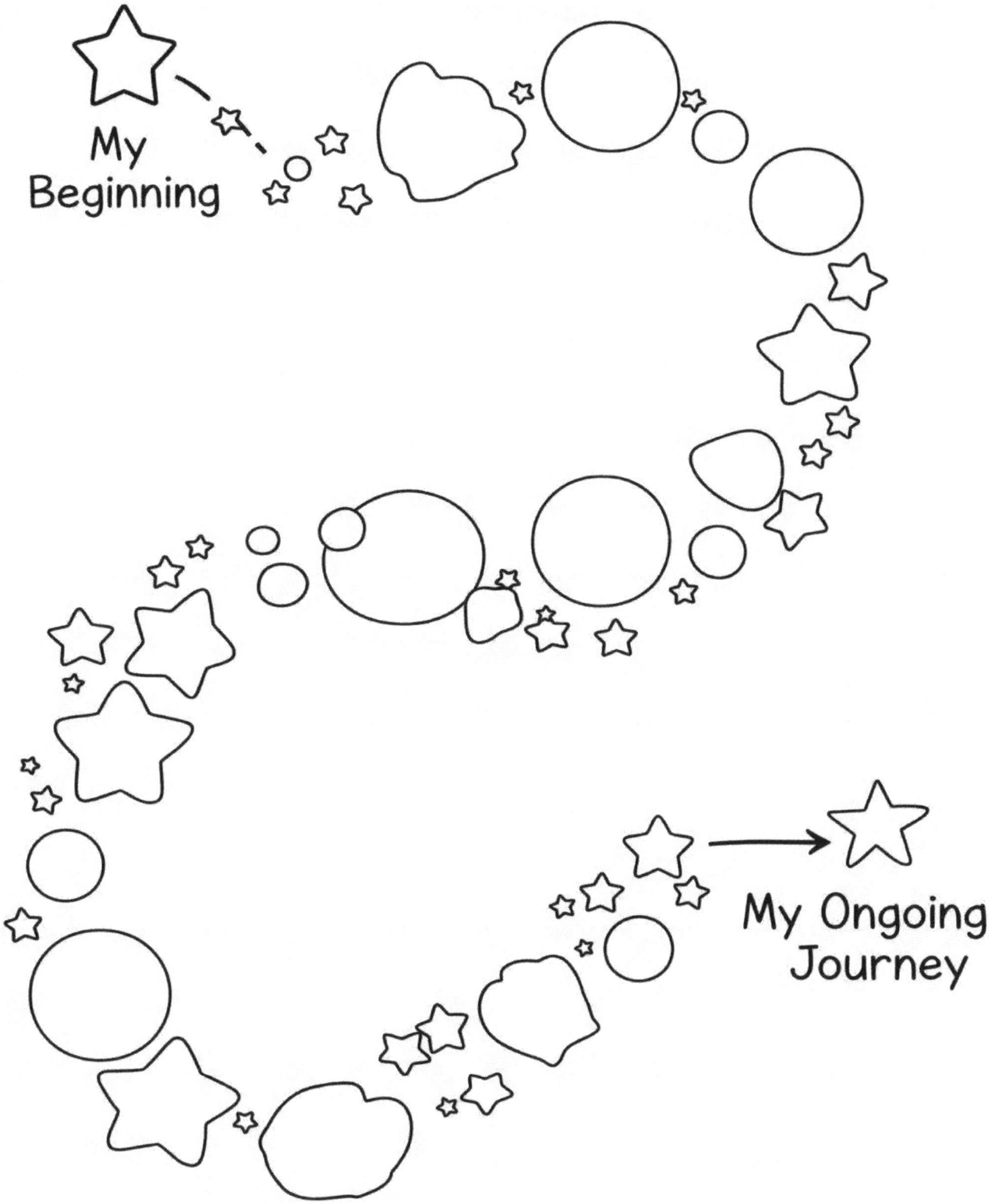

Young Explorers (Grades K-2)
Kindness Constellation Word Search

```
G W M C P O Y H H F S A M L K H S V O A
N G Z R P H G G M E Q F Y H B K P W M C
C L O V E W E B P R T P T U H K A J A Y
Y O S D H K K R U Y Y G G Z O D C N E P
H C V Z Y T W A H D N S U N Y A E P M I
L U A R K P F V J G O K F B O M V M N V
G C L L T J M E Y R T D S U H J M T B P
P B E I M C I Y A D U K A U O Y T S C X
O Q K G M H H M U R S F D O U F H O N T
H T A Y G X Z P B D I B N Q D W O R R Y
U O E N F J X L E G K C H D I X Y X N E
U G P S G T T O F L I V W U N N W B Z M
J V J E T R L T T Q P K V C A K O W U P
C Z A P Y E Y W A W Z L L P R X I P Y A
T S Q X D P C F B T M B Y H Z O L H L T
S E C K I N D S Z J D E B S C K D U E H
A B K X Z O N L T C L P W B S G L A T Y
Z A J H Z P T Q E A Y L D R F B R W C O
L V F F M I A M B W R A E G Z H C K S E
E P Z O N A H M T I G S R K M C E Y Q T
```

Empathy	Space	Stars	Kind
Worry	Angry	Brave	Fear
Calm	Hope	Love	Sad

Young Explorers (Grades K-2)
Kindness Constellation Word Search

```
G W M C P O Y H H F S A M L K H S V O A
N G Z R P H G G M E Q F Y H B K P W M C
C L O V E W E B P R T P T U H K A J A Y
Y O S D H K K R U Y Y G G Z O D C N E P
H C V Z Y T W A H D N S U N Y A E P M I
L U A R K P F V J G O K F B O M V M N V
G C L L T J M E Y R T D S U H J M T B P
P B E I M C I Y A D U K A U O Y T S C X
O Q K G M H H M U R S F D O U F H O N T
H T A Y G X Z P B D I B N Q D W O R R Y
U O E N F J X L E G K C H D I X Y X N E
U G P S G T T O F L I V W U N N W B Z M
J V J E T R L T T Q P K V C A K O W U P
C Z A P Y E Y W A W Z L L P R X I P Y A
T S Q X D P C F B T M B Y H Z O L H L T
S E C K I N D S Z J D E B S C K D U E H
A B K X Z O N L T C L P W B S G L A T Y
Z A J H Z P T Q E A Y L D R F B R W C O
L V F F M I A M B W R A E G Z H C K S E
E P Z O N A H M T I G S R K M C E Y Q T
```

Empathy	Space	Stars	Kind
Worry	Angry	Brave	Fear
Calm	Hope	Love	Sad

Middle Navigators (Grades 3-5)
Kindness Constellation Word Search

```
M V Z J V M K L W J I C E X K P Y Z A M K I X C M X H L J Z
W O R R I O N S G V H N Z T O O T P W S G M Q T J V B S A L
C T V U J V W U D U C S P J M J F K I Y R X A M M C F Q M A
X F L A M M A S O H X J R Z V W O N C N P G Z Y T Q H H W Z
J B V D I E L X P I N M V V E W B Y D X T C H G W T F I U H
S A Q L B L N C S Y Y R E Y J M V X H I Q U G S W D Y M R R
J C Q P Z W J H P T Z G C U J O A A C B R F I R I Z J L T I
N T G S W R H G X C G R Y X K M D K Y W J I R T M M G X O B
U O R Q B I P D H A O V Z I H S C U V Y G Y E L I Z U K I G
P G A Q I H U B D S H N H O L I S T I C B A S Q M O W R L C
Z Y T J V M R R Q L H V S X N Z S Y S N Z T I X Z L N J G O
R I I S R P P W F H M W I T J X S F G X H G L L I B U Q Y P
G P T U W E O S W Y I M Y V E A W E Z K Z F I T C C Y X B B
J T U J I U S F Y P C N F V P L W N R C U H E T V O Q I N Y
W K D M N F E S X M C Z U K A C L Q W U W P N M B M Q W K U
M H E B S L F X U Q P A C A B K G A Z F P P C V F P G X J V
J N X M E X U L P C Z H O A J Z D R T C S T E J A A L W O F
C O F X S A L J L L X U O K U X M Y O I K X I Y B S R G M T
N U D S F A Y N U G R X R N R Z N U W U O I D O G S N H R N
K J M N L R Y A V Y J H R D Y E P Z U M N N N U N I Z U P I
C N G Z X H X R I H C O R D I U M D A D B D X D S J I S X G
Z A H Z Z A R Y A X Z T D Z R D B F L X N R I U N A R Y M E
W L C R V V P P L U C O M P A S S I O N E J X N U E P K Y X
H R I J P C J T H G M A K V M Q R K K Z P M H Q G Y S P E Q
I B Y R E G U L A T E P O P K B Z I Z A L Z P M U C F S S Z
M U W S H A W Q Y O S B T L S R H S B Q D A M A N F Z Y V T
S Z T T R J M O V K I N E C P T D B U D B R Y C T O H I M E
Y P N W U K X H E A L W H T R N Z Y S D G Y Y U Y H K K Y C
D Z Z Q O K M Y Y P X P R S B I Z T Y L V V U Q F K Y B I M
Y A S E S N E R V O U S S G P C T K N U B G U B R O W Z D U
```

Constellation	Compassion	Resilience
Purposeful	Intuition	Grounding
Worrions	Symphony	Regulate
Holistic	Eruption	Kindness
Gratitude	Cordium	Empathy
Nervous	Compass	Whimsy
Flamma	Pluvia	

Middle Navigators (Grades 3-5)
Kindness Constellation Word Search

M V Z J V M K L W J I C E X K P Y Z A M K I X C M X H L J Z
W O R R I O N S G V H N Z T O O T P W S G M Q T J V B S A L
C T V U J V W U D U C S P J M J F K I Y R X A M M C F Q M A
X F L A M M A S O H X J R Z V W O N C N P G Z Y T Q H H W Z
J B V D I E L X P I N M V V E W B Y D X T C H G W T F I U H
S A Q L B L N C S Y Y R E Y J M V X H I Q U G S W D Y M R R
J C Q P Z W J H P T Z G C U J O A A C B R F I R I Z J L T I
N T G S W R H G X C G R Y X K M D K Y W J I R T M M G X O B
U O R Q B I P D H A O V Z I H S C U V Y G Y E L I Z U K I G
P G A Q I H U B D S H N H O L I S T I C B A S Q M O W R L C
Z Y T J V M R R Q L H V S X N Z S Y S N Z T I X Z L N J G O
R I I S R P P W F H M W I T J X S F G X H G L L I B U Q Y P
G P T U W E O S W Y I M Y V E A W E Z K Z F I T C C Y X B B
J T U J I U S F Y P C N F V P L W N R C U H E T V O Q I N Y
W K D M N F E S X M C Z U K A C L Q W U W P N M B M Q W K U
M H E B S L F X U Q P A C A B K G A Z F P P C V F P G X J V
J N X M E X U L P C Z H O A J Z D R T C S T E J A A L W O F
C O F X S A L J L L X U O K U X M Y O I K X I Y B S R G M T
N U D S F A Y N U G R X R N R Z N U W U O I D O G S N H R N
K J M N L R Y A V Y J H R D Y E P Z U M N N N U N I Z U P I
C N G Z X H X R I H C O R D I U M D A D B D X D S J I S X G
Z A H Z Z A R Y A X Z T D Z R D B F L X N R I U N A R Y M E
W L C R V V P P L U C O M P A S S I O N E J X N U E P K Y X
H R I J P C J T H G M A K V M Q R K K Z P M H Q G Y S P E Q
I B Y R E G U L A T E P O P K B Z I Z A L Z P M U C F S S Z
M U W S H A W Q Y O S B T L S R H S B Q D A M A N F Z Y V T
S Z T T R J M O V K I N E C P T D B U D B R Y C T O H I M E
Y P N W U K X H E A L W H T R N Z Y S D G Y Y U Y H K K Y C
D Z Z Q O K M Y Y P X P R S B I Z T Y L V V U Q F K Y B I M
Y A S E S N E R V O U S S G P C T K N U B G U B R O W Z D U

Constellation	Compassion	Resilience
Purposeful	Intuition	Grounding
Worrions	Symphony	Regulate
Holistic	Eruption	Kindness
Gratitude	Cordium	Empathy
Nervous	Compass	Whimsy
Flamma	Pluvia	

You are
AMAZING!
Take care of
YOU!

My Inner Guide Journal Page

The universe needs you. YOU are amazing!